THE COMPLETE

PORTRAIT
PAINTING

COURSE

THE COMPLETE
PORTRAIT
PAINTING
COURSE

ANGELA GAIR

Crescent Books
New York

Design: Hans Verkroost
Editor: Alison Franks
Production: Peter Phillips, Sarah Schuman

This 1990 edition is published by Crescent Books,
distributed by Crown Publishers, Inc.,
225 Park Avenue South, New York, New York 10003

Edited and designed by the Artists House Division
of Mitchell Beazley International Ltd
Artists House, 14–15 Manette Street, London W1V 5LB

ISBN 0-517-68359-8

Typeset by Hourds Typographica, Stafford
Reproduction by La Cromolito s.n.c., Milan
Printed and bound in Portugal by Printer Portuguesa Grafica Lda.

hgfedcba

CONTENTS

INTRODUCTION	6	APPROACHING THE SUBJECT	62
		Keeping a Sketchbook	64
HISTORY AND BACKGROUND	8	Composing the Portrait	66
		The Pose	70
MATERIALS AND EQUIPMENT	12	Lighting	72
Oil Paints and Equipment	14	Clothing	76
Watercolour	18	Informal Portraits	78
Charcoal and Pencil	22	Portraits of Women	80
Pastels	24	Portraits of Men	84
Crayons	26	Children's Portraits	88
Easels	28	Portraits of Older People	92
		Double and Group Portraits	96
TECHNIQUES	30	Self-Portraits	98
Drawing the Head	32	Portraits Outdoors	100
Facial Features	36	Working from Photographs	102
Capturing a Likeness	44		
Using Colour – Flesh Tones	46		
Oil Painting	48	Storage and Presentation	106
Watercolour	52	Glossary	108
Charcoal and Pencil	56	Index	110
Pastel and Crayons	58		

INTRODUCTION

"A portrait is a painting in which there is something wrong with the mouth." The wry humour of this remark, attributed to Whistler, will strike a chord with any artist, professional or amateur. For there is no doubt that painting or drawing a portrait of a fellow human being is one of the most demanding subjects to tackle. You can pretend that the tree you have painted is something like the actual tree, but it is much more difficult to overlook the defects when comparing a portrait to the actual person.

Yet few painting subjects can give both artist and sitter such pleasure when the outcome is successful, and indeed the desire to paint or draw a face so that it can be recognized as a particular individual is an instinct as old as human history. As the Elizabethan portraitist Nicholas Hilliard put it, "Of all things, the perfection is to imitate the face of mankind."

Portraits demand the ability to create a solid, lifelike head and features that are a recognizable likeness of the sitter. The secret is the keen observation and analysis of the features *you* consider characterize the sitter, whether it be a strong jawline, a prominent nose, or large eyes. The human face is not as perfectly symmetrical as it might at first appear, and identifying these minute differences can also help to produce a good likeness.

But the reproduction of the features alone does not necessarily reveal a great deal about the subject. What makes a portrait memorable is the ability of the artist to get "under the skin" of the sitter, to reveal the living, breathing person behind the outer shell. Portraits by such masters as da Vinci, Rembrandt, Gainsborough and Picasso are extremely diverse in style and execution, but the quality they all have in common is a spiritual insight into their subjects which goes far beyond a mere superficial resemblance of the features. These portraits – of people unknown to us – have the power to move us deeply, often centuries after they were first painted, because we perceive the sympathy and understanding that existed between artist and sitter. The ability to express the character, personality and temperament of your subject is the extra ingredient that makes a good portrait into fine art. It cannot be taught, but is a result of instinct and insight. From the outset, it is important to establish a rapport with your sitter and to make him or her feel relaxed. Many painters talk as they work, encouraging their sitters to do the same, and this helps bring a natural and animated expression to the subject's face. Most people have characteristic gestures that, used in relaxed conversation, help to reveal their personalities.

Portrait painting is likely to make the most demands on the artist, but it also offers some of the greatest rewards. Whatever your level of painting experience, I hope that in this book you will find the ideas, the techniques and the inspiration you need to start creating stronger, more expressive likenesses than ever before.

Angela Gair

HISTORY AND BACKGROUND

Portraits often tell us as much about the times in which they were painted as about the person portrayed, and the sheer number and variety of portraits drawn and painted over the centuries provide a fascinating source of imagery as well as bringing the past to life.

According to the first century writer, Pliny, the very earliest painting was a profile portrait made by tracing the outline of a man's shadow on a wall. Yet portraiture as it is understood today was a relatively late arrival in the history of art, only really beginning in earnest in the 15th century. The Ancient Greeks and Romans considered portrait *sculpture* to be the finest art form, though the few painted likenesses of the period still in existence are of equal quality. With the fall of Rome and the rise of Christianity the tradition of portraiture declined. Religious dogma decreed that there should be no graven images, and kings, queens and saints were portrayed as stylized emblems of authority rather than as actual people. The 14th century saw a gradual liberation of attitude, however, and Giotto di Bondone (c.1267–1337) was the first painter to break with convention and portray real human beings.

In Italy and Flanders, the flowering of the Renaissance in the 15th and 16th centuries had a profound influence on Western art, and its reverberations are still felt today. The term Renaissance means "rebirth" and this new era saw the narrow, superstitious beliefs of the Middle Ages give way to a spirit of intellectual enquiry and the rebirth of interest in the humanist philosophies of Ancient Greece and Rome. Painters and sculptors re-asserted the dignity of man, and the rapid development of theories of perspective and proportion led to an even-greater realism in figure painting. Before the Renaissance, portraits had shown either a full-frontal or a profile view, but mastery of the three-quarter face, initiated by Netherlandish artists in the first half of the 15th century, was a crucial development in the history of portraiture. Jan van Eyck (c.1384–1441) was the first to introduce the idea of illuminating the far side of the sitter's head in the three-quarter pose, rather than the near side; here, because the contours of the near side were modelled by shadows, the illusion of form and depth was

Above: *The Arnolfini Marriage* displays Jan van Eyck's originality in his pursuit of flawless reality, his understanding of narrative composition, and his mastery of the recently refined oils. The couple are seen making their vows, and van Eyck ingeniously reflects the scene in the mirror behind.

Right: Vermeer, whose pictures were hardly known until the late 19th century, was the greatest of the Dutch masters at conveying the effects of falling light. In *The* *Girl with a Red Hat*, the model's features are rendered with a soft translucency that seems to glow from within the flesh, rather than to strike it from without.

enhanced. Albrecht Dürer (1471–1528) and Hans Holbein (1497–1543) similarly displayed superb draughtsmanship and mastery of form through the use of *chiaroscuro* – modulations of light and dark – and in Italy, Michelangelo (1475–1564), Raphael (1483–1520) and Leonardo da Vinci (1452–1519) developed these techniques to even further heights of excellence. Leonardo, of course, left us the most famous portrait of all time – the *Mona Lisa*. Generation after generation has sought the secret of her enigmatic smile. Leonardo also introduced the technique of *sfumato*, the softening and dissolving of forms to create "lost and found" passages where parts of the figure appear to merge into the background, thus deepening the mystery.

The materials and pigments available were also improving at this time. Jan van Eyck played a major role in pioneering the use of oil paint, which began to supplant *tempera* and *fresco* as the major medium. The technique was brought to Venice by Antonello da Messina (*c.*1430–1479) and the Italians marvelled at the range of tone and blending and the smooth, glass-like finish obtainable with this new medium.

In northern Europe, the great age of portraiture was the 17th century, largely due to the patronage of a new class of rich merchants who commissioned portraits of themselves in professional attire usually surrounded by the accroutements of their wealth. Oil paint was being more widely used and the laying of transparent glazes, one on top of the other, allowed artists to paint with a luminosity that captured the quality of flesh tones as well as the sparkle of jewels and the sheen of satin and pearls. At the same time, artists such as Caravaggio (1573–1610) developed a freer style of paint handling, in which the brushmarks themselves were an expressive and integral part of the image. Caravaggio combined a vigorous and uncompromising realism with a heightened *chiaroscuro* that conveyed an impression of intense drama.

This was to be a major influence on the work of Rembrandt van Rijn (1606–1669). Rembrandt, as well as being the greatest interpreter of the human spirit in the history of painting, was also among the greatest pioneers of the oil painting technique. He pushed the medium to its limits, building up thick impastos to suggest textures such as the wrinkled skin of an old face or the frothy white lace of a collar, while many overlapping glazes were used to produce rich depths of tone. He was a master of *chiaroscuro*; by cloaking his figures in a veil of shadows and half-lights, he used the power of suggestion to imbue his portraits with tenderness and emotion.

The 18th century was a time of peace and prosperity in England, and this was reflected in the informality and intimacy of portraits of the time. Aristocrats and country squires were great patrons of the arts and commissioned portraits of themselves enjoying the pleasures of life in the country, surrounded by their families, their dogs and horses. Thomas Gainsborough (1727–1788) was a skilled recorder of his times, and his portraits of the gentry, often in an open-air setting, have a lyrical charm and casual grace. Sir Joshua Reynolds (1723–1792) preferred to paint actors and men of letters, while William Hogarth (1697–1764) exposed the hypocrisy of contemporary society in his satirical pictures.

The 19th century was a time of great social upheaval in Europe, and this was reflected in the diverse portrait styles which evolved. The French painter Dominique Ingres (1780–1867) worked in the Classical tradition, immortalizing his patrons with superb skill and a certain cool detachment. In complete contrast, the Impressionists rejected the conventions of Classicism and their portraits were determinedly informal, depicting ordinary people doing mundane things. They also introduced the "direct" or "*alla prima*" technique; instead of completing the painting stage by stage with successive layers of glazes and scumbles, they built up a mosaic of patches of pure colour in order to capture a sense of flickering, quivering light on hair, skin and clothing.

At the beginning of this century the Cubists, the Fauves and the Expressionists rebelled against the tradition of attempted realism altogether, and the portrait, too, became a vehicle for social commentary or for stylistic experiment. In a reaction to the horrors of war and the alienating effects of a fast-changing society, artists became less concerned with outer appearances and more concerned with the expression of the inner man, his fears and emotions, using heightened colour and deliberate distortions of form.

Traditional portrait painting remains a vital and fascinating subject, however, and the urge to depict the complexity and uniqueness of the human character is as compelling now as it has ever been.

Left: *A Tramp* by John Singer Sargent. Few painters have surpassed Sargent's ability to deal with surface realities of form and texture, yet at the same time to penetrate beneath the surface to catch a characteristic gesture or fleeting expression that bring a portrait alive. This watercolour is painted with an apparently casual touch, yet the dignity of the old man's direct gaze stays in the memory.

Below: *An Evening in the Vale* is one of the small "conversation pieces" which Henry Tonks painted toward the end of his career. This group portrait features George Moore reading to Mr and Mrs John Hutchinson, Wilson Steer (asleep) and Tonks himself (by the fireplace). The painting is a fine example of the use of counterchange (the placing of light areas against dark, and dark against light) as a compositional element to lead the eye through the picture.

Top left: *Portrait of the Artist's Wife* shows the grace and tenderness of observation typical of Thomas Gainsborough's portraits, as well as the astonishing variety of his impulsive brushwork. Gainsborough's real sympathies lay with landscape painting, and he constantly referred in his letters to the "curs'd Face Business". Yet he accepted that to make a living in 18th-century England an artist was obliged to paint portraits, and he made a great success of it.

Bottom left: Ingres was very much concerned with composition and the way it influences the mood of a portrait. In *Monsieur Bertin*, we have a strong, triangular composition which is weighted in the lower half, giving an impression of solidity. Bertin's hands are not relaxed but flexed, as if he is on the verge of rising from his seat. Each of these elements is designed to reflect elements of the sitter's character.

MATERIALS
AND
EQUIPMENT

A trip to an art supply store can be both exciting and daunting. With such a vast range of materials and equipment available, how do you make an informed choice about what is essential to your needs and what is not? While it is important to experiment with various media, you don't want to start with an ill-chosen collection of costly items that will serve only to confuse and inhibit you. It is worth remembering that some of the greatest works of art have been done with basic materials and a mere handful of colours. It is important to choose a medium that is both compatible with the subject you have in mind and which suits your style of working. This section discusses a range of media and equipment for use in drawing and painting portraits, and explains their various characteristics. There is also practical advice on how to stretch watercolour paper, how to prepare canvas, and choosing the best colours to start off with.

The materials used in the assembly of hog's hair and bristle brushes.

OIL PAINTS AND EQUIPMENT

Contrary to popular belief, you don't need a vast amount of elaborate and expensive equipment to begin in oil painting. A dozen tubes of colour, a few brushes and a sheet of canvas or board are the basic requirements, plus a palette, a medium for thinning the paint, and turpentine for cleaning brushes. As you become more proficient, you can add to your armoury of equipment as the need arises.

Oil paints are sold in tubes and are available in two different grades: "Artists" and "Students". Artists' colours are of better quality and this is reflected in the price. They are made from the finest pigments ground with a minimum of oil so their consistency is stiff, and the colours retain their brilliance well on exposure to light.

Students' colours are labelled with a trade name such as "Georgian" (Rowney) or "Winton" (Winsor & Newton). These paints are much cheaper because they contain lower-quality pigments. They also have a greater oil content, so they are more "floppy" in consistency. They are, however, perfectly adequate for beginners. As you become more proficient in the medium, you can change to the better grade.

The range of oil colours in art supply stores is bewildering. Some are indispensable, but many are not essential as similar colours can be obtained by mixing. For the beginner I would recommend a limited palette of 12 or so colours, the following being good all-rounders: cadmium red, light red, yellow ochre, cadmium yellow, cobalt blue, French Ultramarine, terre verte, raw umber, raw sienna, burnt umber, burnt sienna, flake white, ivory black.

Brushes

Oil painting brushes come in a wide range of sizes and shapes. Each makes a different kind of mark, but some are more versatile than others. Through experiment you will find which ones are best suited to your own painting style.

Bristle brushes are the most popular and versatile. The best quality ones are made of stiff, white hog bristles with split ends that hold a lot of paint. Sable brushes, the most expensive, are used for smoother, softer and more precise brushwork, and for applying glazes. Their fine points are ideal for delicate passages and linear details. Nylon brushes are cheap and hard-wearing, but lack the "spring" of natural bristles and lose their points quickly.

Brush types

Rounds are thin, long-bristled brushes that taper slightly at the ends. This is the most versatile brush shape, especially for portrait work. It covers large areas quickly and is useful for sketching in outlines.

Filberts are similar to rounds but fuller in the middle. They are available with long bristles or short, and make soft, tapering strokes.

Flats have square ends and long bristles that hold a lot of paint. They make long, fluid strokes and are useful for blending. The square end of the brush is capable of making fine lines.

Brights are the same as flats, but with shorter bristles that make strongly textured strokes. The stiff bristles are useful for applying thick, heavy paint to produce impasto effects.

Each type of brush comes in a range of sizes, from 00 (the smallest) to no. 12 (the largest). The brush size you choose will depend on the scale and style of your paintings. In general, it is better to start with medium to large brushes as they cover large areas quickly but can also be employed for small touches.

The best-quality brushes are always worth the extra expense, as they last longer and produce a far more satisfying mark.

All brushes should be thoroughly cleaned after use. Rinse off the paint with turpentine or white spirit and wipe with a rag. Then clean the bristles with mild soap and lukewarm water, rubbing the brush around gently in your palm. It is essential to remove all the paint that accumulates at the neck of the ferrule. If paint hardens here, the bristles will splay out. Rinse the brush well, shake it out and smooth it into shape, then leave to dry naturally, head upwards.

Palettes

The traditional oil painter's palette is oval or rectangular in shape and made of wood. It is designed for easel painting, with a thumbhole and indentation at one end so that the artist can hold the palette comfortably in one hand while painting with the other hand.

It is essential to treat a new wooden palette with linseed oil before you use it, to seal the wood and make it non-absorbent. This will prevent the oil paint from sinking into the wood, causing it to dry out too quickly on the palette. Rub a coating of oil into both sides of the palette and leave it for several days until it has fully penetrated the grain of the wood.

If you prefer to have both hands free while painting, a table top palette can be placed on a nearby surface. For general studio use a large sheet of glass, plastic or wood will suffice, and can be made as large as you like for mixing large quantities of paint.

Disposable paper palettes made of oil-proof paper are sold in pads with tear-off sheets. These are useful for outdoor work or if you are in a hurry, as they save time when cleaning up.

Mediums

The consistency of oil paint as it comes from the tube may be just right for use if you paint very thickly, but more often it needs to be thinned to make it easier to apply to the canvas. The most commonly used painting medium is a mixture of linseed oil and genuine gum turpentine, usually in the proportions of 60 per cent oil to 40 per cent turpentine. For a thicker consistency which dries more quickly you can add a little varnish or stand oil to the medium.

Other equipment

None of the items listed below is essential, but you may find some of them useful.

Painting knives have flexible, springy blades and cranked handles, and can be used to apply paint directly to the support and for certain techniques such as *impasto* (see page 50). They are also used to scrape away wet paint when making alterations to the picture. You can use the tip of the blade for making fine details, and the side for blending or hard-edged marks.

Palette knives are broader than painting knives and have flat handles. They, too, are sometimes used for applying paint direct on to the support, and they are useful also for mixing paint on the palette and for scraping paint off the palette at the end of a painting session.

Dippers are small metal cups made to hold oil and turpentine and which clip onto the edge of the palette. These are not essential – you can

just as easily keep small jars of painting medium on a nearby surface.

Mahl stick This is traditionally a long cane with a chamois tip at one end, though modern-day ones are made of aluminium with a rubber tip. It is a great help for steadying your painting arm when doing detailed, controlled work. The end of the stick is held in one hand so that it crosses the painting diagonally with the tip resting on a dry section of the work. The painting arm can then be rested on the stick.

Canvases and boards

Canvas is available in various weights and in fine, medium and coarse-grained textures. If your painting style uses bold, heavy brushstrokes, a coarsely-woven texture is best. For detailed brushwork and soft blending, a smooth, finely woven texture is more suitable.

Most art supply stores offer several grades of canvas, either glued on to stiff board, ready-stretched, or sold by the yard on a roll. Below is a guide to what is available.

Linen is considered the best canvas. It has a fine, even grain that is free of knots, is very durable, and retains its tautness when stretched on a frame. It is, however, the most expensive.

Cotton canvas is about half the price of linen and is a perfectly adequate painting surface on which to experiment. However, the texture quickly becomes obscured by layers of paint and the surface becomes rather flat. Most cotton weaves stretch poorly and they do not take primer as well as linen.

Canvases composed of mixed fibres such as linen/cotton should be avoided as they stretch unevenly.

Canvas can be bought ready-primed and stretched on wooden frames in various sizes. The surface of such a canvas is taut but flexible, with a pleasant receptiveness to the stroke of the brush.

Commercially prepared canvas boards are suitable for beginners trying out oils for the first time. However, the surface is hard and unyielding, with a rather mechanical texture and a slippery surface.

Oil sketching paper is specially prepared so that oil paint will not sink into the surface. Available in pads with tear-off sheets, it is particularly useful for practice work.

Right: Canvas is available in a wide range of textures, from smooth to rough. Try out several different types until you find one that suits you best.

Left: A range of oil canvas papers and (inset) ready-stretched and primed canvases, available in a variety of sizes.

WATERCOLOURS

There are two grades of watercolour paint available – "Artists" and "Students". The students range is cheaper, but the quality of the paints is noticeably inferior, so they are a false economy. Only those paints labelled "Artists" colours can be relied upon to give the richness of colour, the glow and transparency that the keen artist requires.

Watercolour paints are sold in several forms: pans or half pans of semi-moist colour; cakes of dry colour; tubes of thick moist colour; and bottles of liquid colour.

Tubes

Watercolour in tube form is popular and easy to use, and the quality of the paint is very good. The only drawback is that it is easy to squeeze out more paint than you need onto your palette, and the paint will leak and solidify if the cap isn't replaced properly after use. It is best to squeeze out only a few colours at a time, keeping them well apart so that there is no danger of them running together if you use too much water when mixing.

Pans and half pans

These small blocks of semi-moist watercolour can be bought individually as well as in special watercolour boxes with slots to hold the pans in place and a lid which opens out to form a convenient mixing palette. They are economical to buy and convenient for use out of doors as they are easily portable. However, it does sometimes take a little effort to lift enough colour onto the brush to make a large wash.

Dry cakes

These are seldom used nowadays. Although they are the least expensive to buy, these round discs of pigment require much scrubbing with a wet brush before yielding their colour.

Bottles

Bottled watercolours are concentrated and come complete with eyedroppers so that they can easily be transferred to the palette. Just a few drops in a saucer of water produces enough colour for a large, expansive wash. However, the colours tend to be rather vivid and some dye the paper so strongly that they are impossible to lift out.

Permanence

All watercolours will fade eventually if exposed for too long to sunlight. Due to the nature of the individual pigments used, however, some colours are more permanent than others. All reputable manufacturers classify their paints in four degrees of permanence:

Class AA   extremely permanent
Class A   durable
Class B   moderately durable
Class C   fugitive

The majority of colours fall into the second category. Fugitive colours – unfortunately these

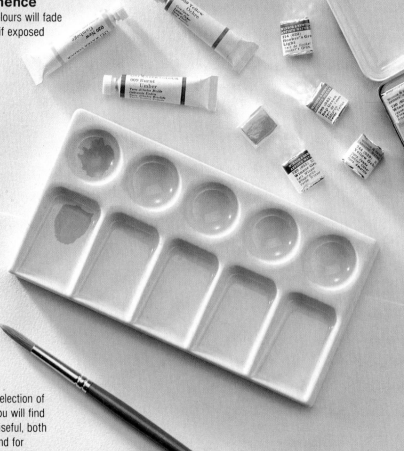

Watercolours are available in sets as well as in individual pans and tubes. The boxes fold out to double as palettes. Bottled, concentrated watercolour incorporates an eye-dropper applicator. Tube colours have to be squeezed onto the palette and mixed with water. Ceramic or plastic palettes have several wells to prevent colours flowing together. As well as a selection of three or four brushes you will find small natural sponges useful, both for applying the paint and for mopping it up if it runs too much.

include such luscious colours as carmine and rose madder – fade away in a short time and are generally best avoided altogether.

Colours

Most subjects can be tackled with a palette of ten or 12 colours. It is best to stick to an even more restricted palette to start with, as this forces you to consider the basics of colour mixing and also imposes a pleasing harmony and unity on the finished work. As you gain more experience you may add more colours, or you may possibly discard some. While there is no definitive palette (everyone has their own pet favourites) the following colours should meet most requirements: cadmium red, alizarin

crimson, yellow ochre, cerulean blue, burnt umber, Paynes grey, ivory black, cadmium yellow, Hooker's green, ultramarine, burnt sienna, Indian red.

Brushes

Brushes are especially important in watercolour painting, so don't stint on them. The best red sable brushes are expensive, but they give the best results and will last for many years. They are resilient, hold their shape well and have a life and springiness which results in lively, yet controlled brushstrokes.

Slightly less expensive are sable blends – sable mixed with other hairs, such as squirrel or ox hair. Cheaper still are synthetic (nylon) brushes, and brushes made with squirrel or ox hair alone, but they rarely give good results; they quickly lose their shape, the hairs tend to drop out, and they don't have the springiness of sable brushes. However, the cost of a large sable brush for laying on washes may be prohibitive, so ox hair is the best alternative here.

Three or four brushes are enough to start with and your initial

selection should include large and small brushes, and flat and round ones. In addition to brushes, a small natural sponge will come in handy for blotting paint and making textures.

Look after your brushes and they will last you well. Never use a brush to scrub at the paint and do not leave brushes standing in water while you work. Always rinse the brush in clean water after use, then reshape it either by pulling it between your lips or by gently drawing it over the palm of your hand, moulding the hairs to a point. Stand your brushes, hairs uppermost, in a jar. If storing brushes in a box, ensure that they are dry, otherwise mildew will set in and spoil them.

Watercolour paper

A wide variety of watercolour paper is available, both in single sheets and in pads and blocks. Paper varies in surface texture, in weight (the thickness of the sheets) in colour and in size. Your choice of paper is a matter of personal preference, depending very much upon your own style of painting and the particular subject in question. Start by buying single sheets of various types and try them out – you will soon

discover which ones "feel" right for you.

Choosing the right kind of paper is important to a watercolour painter, as its surface texture plays an active role in the making of a picture. A rough-textured paper, for example, breaks up the brush strokes as they are applied, adding a touch of spontaneity and liveliness. The very best watercolour papers are handmade by skilled craftsmen. They are made from pure linen rag which has been specially processed to eliminate impurities. Handmade papers are coated on one side only with a size that is extremely receptive to watercolour. This side is recognized by holding the paper up to the light and shows the maker's watermark the right way round.

The surface texture of the paper is known as its "tooth". There are three kinds of surface:

Hot pressed is very smooth, with almost no tooth. It is suitable for finely detailed work, but most artists find its surface too slippery for pure watercolour painting.

Not (meaning not hot pressed, and sometimes referred to as "cold pressed"). This paper is the one most generally used by artists and is ideal for less experienced painters. Its medium-textured surface is good for both large, smooth washes and for fine brush detailing.

Sable round brushes

Bright – square synthetic brush

Synthetic round brushes

Fan blender brush

Stretching paper

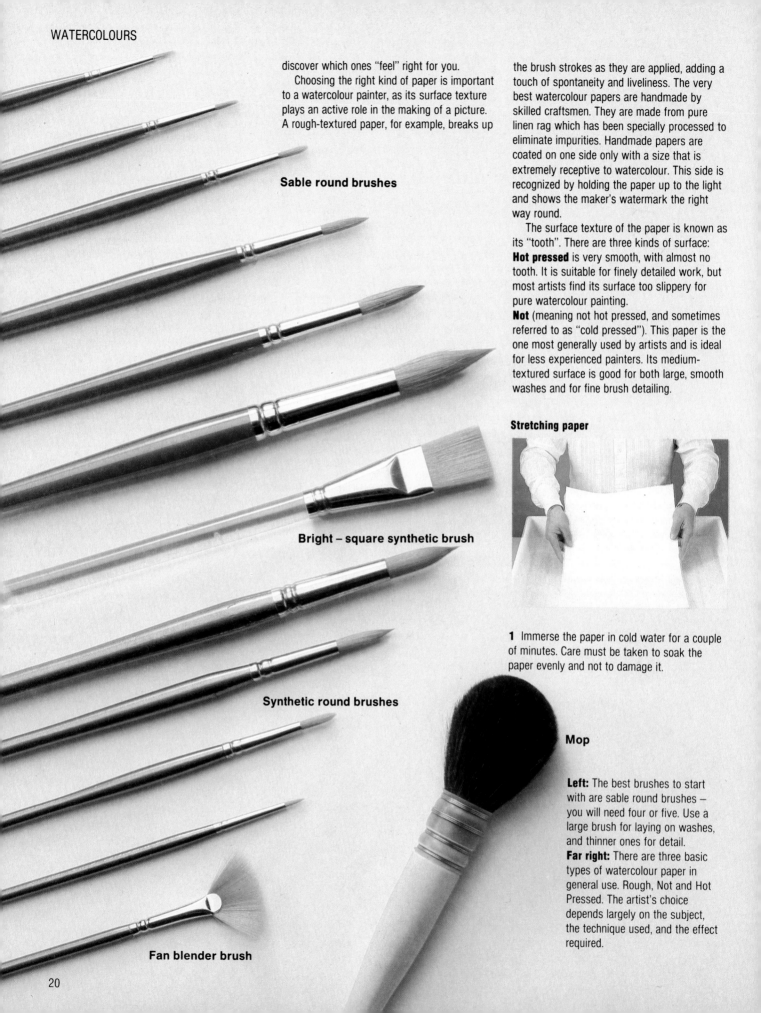

1 Immerse the paper in cold water for a couple of minutes. Care must be taken to soak the paper evenly and not to damage it.

Mop

Left: The best brushes to start with are sable round brushes – you will need four or five. Use a large brush for laying on washes, and thinner ones for detail.

Far right: There are three basic types of watercolour paper in general use. Rough, Not and Hot Pressed. The artist's choice depends largely on the subject, the technique used, and the effect required.

Rough paper has a pronounced "tooth" to its surface, which catches at the brush and causes a watercolour wash to break up. The paint sinks into the pitted surface and leaves speckles untouched, producing a luminous sparkle through the wash. However, beginners may find it difficult to control the paint on a rough paper, so a certain amount of practice may be necessary.

Weights

Traditionally, the weight of paper refers to the weight of a ream, which is 480 sheets. Thus a paper referred to as 72lbs is a thin paper, 480 sheets of which weigh 72lbs. The lightest watercolour paper is 72lbs, the heaviest 400lbs. Under the metric system, weight is measured in grams per square metre (gsm). Thus a paper referred to as 100gsm is a thin paper, one square metre of which weighs 100 grams. The heaviest paper weighs 640 grams per square metre.

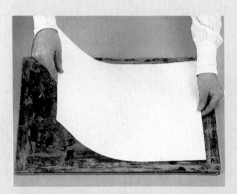

2 Hold the paper up to dislodge any surplus water. Then lay it flat on the board. Remove any air bubbles by rubbing briskly outward from the centre.

3 Stick down the edges of the paper with strips of dampened gummed tape. As the paper dries it will shrink and become taut.

Waterford Rough

Waterford Not

Waterford HP

Whatman Rough

Whatman Not

Whatman HP

Bloxworthy Not

Bloxworthy Rough

Bockingford

Georgian

Cartridge

Stretching

For watercolour painting, lightweight papers, say up to 285gsm (140lbs) should be stretched before use, to prevent them "cockling" or buckling when paint and water are applied. The paper is soaked in water, expands, and is then fastened down securely to a board. As the paper dries it shrinks as taut as a drum. Properly stretched paper will not buckle, even when flooded with paint and water. With heavier papers, stretching is not usually necessary unless your technique involves a lot of heavy washes.

To save time, you can buy pre-stretched paper in blocks. The sheets of paper are gummed around the edges and can be separated using a palette knife when the painting is finished and dry.

CHARCOAL AND PENCIL

Pencils and charcoal sticks are used for making sketches and preliminary drawings and are expressive and versatile media in their own right, whether for large or small pieces of work.

Charcoal

Charcoal is the oldest drawing medium. Prehistoric man used sticks of charred wood from the fire as a tool to draw the outlines of animals on the walls of caves. Today, artists' charcoal is produced from vine and willow twigs charred in special kilns.

Charcoal is available as natural or compressed sticks, in pencil form, or as a powder. It also comes in various thicknesses and degrees of hardness. Soft charcoal is more powdery and adheres less easily to the paper, so is a good choice if you want to create broad tonal effects. It also smudges easily, so use it with care and spray the finished work with fixative (see page 106). The harder type of charcoal is best for more detailed, linear work as it smudges less easily. Soft charcoal makes a more intense black mark, while harder sticks are good for intermediate grey tones.

Stick charcoal is made from vine or willow twigs. Thin sticks are suitable for sketches and for delicate, detailed work. Thicker ones are better for bold work and for covering large areas quickly. The sticks come in their natural state, so are not uniform in shape.

Compressed charcoal consists of powdered charcoal combined with a binder and compressed into short, thick sticks. It is stronger than stick charcoal and doesn't break so easily, and is also useful for laying in broad blocks of tone.

Charcoal pencils are made from thin sticks of compressed charcoal encased in wood. They are cleaner to handle and easier to control than stick charcoal, and have a harder texture. Only the point can be used, so they cannot produce a broad side stroke, but they make firm lines and strokes and the tip can be sharpened for detailed work. Like ordinary graphite pencils, they come in a range of grades: hard, medium and soft.

Powdered charcoal can be spread across the paper with the fingers or with a *torchon* (a paper stump made from blotting paper rolled up to form a hard, pencil-like implement). Powdered charcoal is ideal for covering large

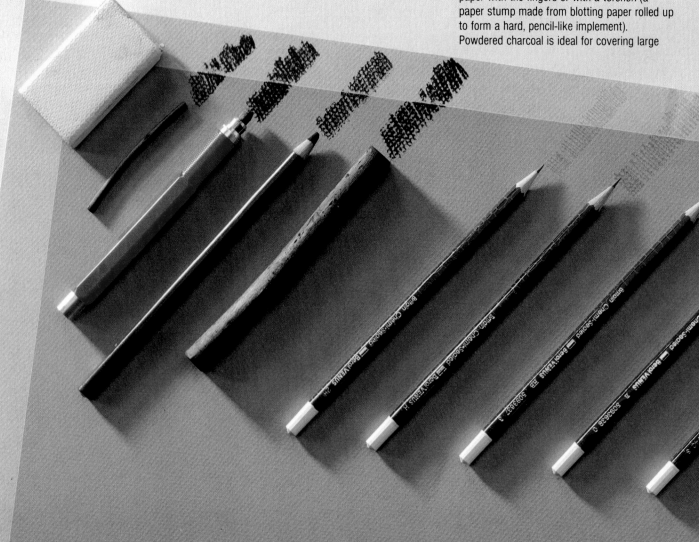

areas. You can obtain a wide range of tones as the more powder is applied the darker the tone. More delicate blending can be accomplished with a *torchon*.

Pencils

The immediacy, versatility and sensitivity of pencils make them the most popular instrument for drawing. Equally capable of producing a quick sketch or a finely worked drawing, the pencil is ideal for capturing the subtle texture of skin and hair in a portrait drawing.

Ordinary wooden pencils contain solid graphite (the term "lead pencil" is a misnomer; when graphite was first discovered in the 16th century it was at first thought to be lead). Pencils are graded by the H and B systems,

according to the relative hardness or softness of the graphite core. Hard pencils range from 9H (the hardest) to H. Soft pencils range from 8B (the softest) to B. HB is midway between hard and soft and is good for everyday use. A very soft lead enables you to make broad, soft lines, while hard leads are suited to fine, precise lines and detail. A medium grade such as a 2B or 3B is probably the most popular and easy for drawing. Also available are extremely soft pencils, which sometimes have a flattened lead. These produce strong, dark marks and are especially effective on rough-textured paper.

Other types of pencil include propelling pencils and clutch pencils, designed to take a range of interchangeable hard and soft leads. These have an advantage over wooden pencils

because they don't need sharpening. Graphite sticks are quite thick and are suitable for working on a large scale.

Use a craft knife or scalpel blade for sharpening pencils; pencil sharpeners often break off the lead just as it is sharpened to a suitable point. A pencil that has been sharpened with a blade will retain its point far longer than one sharpened with a pencil sharpener. For erasing, kneadable or putty erasers are best, as they are cleaner in use than the familiar India rubber and can be moulded to any shape, including a delicate point to pick out a small error.

The different kinds of pencil and charcoal available create a variety of marks on smooth and rough-textured paper. **Below, from left to right:** kneadable eraser, thin vine charcoal, charcoal propelling pencil, compressed charcoal pencil, thick vine charcoal, graphite pencils 2H, H, HB, B, 3B, 6B, Black Beauties, and a rag for blending and smoothing. Shown above these are a sanding block and scalpel, for sharpening.

PASTELS

There is no doubt that pastels are a very seductive medium. Their sumptuous, jewel-like colours are a delight to the eye and they have a soft, luxurious feel as they glide over the paper. In common with all drawing media, pastels offer the satisfaction of immediate contact with the paper and are easy to manipulate.

Pastels are made from finely ground pigments bound together with gum to form a stiff paste, which is then shaped into sticks and allowed to harden. There are four main types available: soft and hard pastels, pastel pencils and oil pastels, and each kind has a different consistency.

Soft pastels
Soft pastels are the most widely used of the various pastel types because they produce the wonderful velvety bloom which is one of the main attractions of pastel art. They contain more pigment and less binder, so the colours are rich and vibrant. The smooth, thick quality of soft pastels produces rich, painterly effects. They are easy to apply, requiring little pressure to make a mark and you can blend and smudge them with your finger, a rag, or a *torchon*.

Hard pastels
These contain less pigment and more binder than the soft type, so although the colours aren't as brilliant they do have a firmer consistency. Hard pastels can be sharpened to a point with a blade and used for crisp lines and details. Unlike soft pastels, they don't crumble and break easily and don't clog the tooth of the paper, so are often used in the preliminary stages of a painting to outline the composition, or for adding details and accents at the end.

Pastel pencils
Thin pastel sticks are available encased in wood, like normal pencils. Pastel pencils are clean to use, don't break or crumble as traditional pastels do, and give greater control of handling. They are perfect for line sketches and detailed or small-scale work, and can be used in conjunction with hard and soft pastels.

Oil pastels

Oil pastels are different in character from traditional pastels. The pigment and chalk are combined with an oil binder instead of gum, making the sticks stronger and harder. Oil pastels make thick, buttery strokes and the colours are clear and brilliant. Though not as easy to control as normal pastels, they have a robust quality which makes them ideal for direct, spontaneous working. The colours can be blended and softened with a brush or rag dipped in turpentine, and the waxy surface can be scratched into with a sharp tool. Oil pastels require little or no fixative as they don't smudge easily.

Choosing colours

Unlike oils and watercolours, pastel colours cannot be premixed on the palette. Instead, the artist uses a range of sticks, each of a different tint or shade, and the colours are laid over each other, juxtaposed, or blended together.

With a range of several hundred colours and many brands available, choosing an initial collection of pastels can seem daunting. Using a small boxed selection is a good way to begin,

but as you gain more experience you may prefer to buy individual sticks. If you are choosing colours for portrait painting, be sure to include a good range of colours for the flesh half-tones and shadows – greys, grey-greens and warm earth colours.

Shown **below** is a selection of chalk pastels and oil pastels and Ingres and Mi-Teintes paper in a variety of colours and textures. Fixative, applied with a mouth spray diffuser (**far right**) ensures that the finished work does not smudge.

CRAYONS

There is a wide range of coloured pencils, crayons and chalks on the market that can be loosely grouped under the heading of crayons. Often thought of as being solely for children's use, crayons are in fact a versatile medium for fine art as well. They are convenient to use, and you can vary your work from bold and intense to delicate and finely detailed.

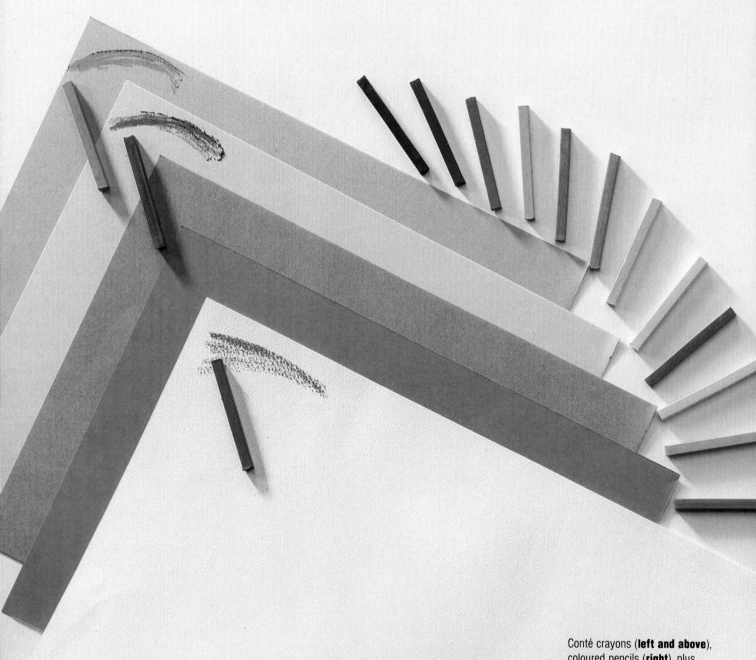

Conté crayons (**left and above**), coloured pencils (**right**), plus a selection of tinted papers. The paper's colour and texture will play an integral part in the finished drawing.

Coloured pencils

Since David Hockney set a precedent with his highly successful series of portraits in coloured pencil, this medium has become increasingly popular with fine artists. Clean, quick and portable, coloured pencils are a very useful sketching and drawing tool. They allow you to work with the accuracy of pencil and at the same time involve colour, and they are soft enough to allow delicate shading while sharpening to a point for controlled lines.

Water-soluble pencils

These are a cross between coloured pencils and watercolour paints. You can apply the colour dry, as you would with an ordinary pencil, and you can also use a soft watercolour brush dipped in water to blend colours together to create a wash-like effect. This facility for producing tightly controlled work and spontaneous marks and loose washes makes

Right: A sensitively rendered portrait drawing in Conté crayon on tinted paper.

water-soluble pencils very flexible and effective for capturing the delicacy of skin tones.

Conté crayons

These are oblong sticks of very high grade compressed chalk, slightly harder and oilier than pastels. Traditionally used for tonal drawings, conté crayons were in the past limited to black, white, grey, and three earth colours — sanguine, sepia and bistre. Recently a wide range of bright and subtle colours has been introduced, available individually or in boxed sets. You can use the flat side of the crayon for shading and creating broad, flat areas of colour, or break off pieces about 2.5cm (1in) long and use a corner or edge to make crisp outlines. Conté crayons combine well with soft pastels and with charcoal, and are shown to their best advantage when used on tinted paper with a fairly rough texture.

Chalks

Chalk is a medium with a long and illustrious history. Some of the most beautiful drawings ever produced — by Michelangelo, Andrea del Sarto, Watteau and Toulouse-Lautrec — were executed in chalk on buff paper. Quarried straight from the ground, chalk is available in a limited range of colours: grey, white, black, red and brown, in pencil or stick form. The pigments are mixed with wax or oil, resulting in a texture slightly harder than that of pastel.

EASELS

Easels provide a firm support for your drawings and paintings. There is a wide selection of easels available in various sizes, weights and styles, and each has been carefully designed with a particular working situation in mind.

Before investing in an easel, which can be an expensive item, you should consider your working preferences. The watercolour painter, for example, will need an easel that can be tilted to a horizontal position so that wet washes can be applied without danger of their running down the paper. Ask yourself some basic questions: which medium do you favour? Do you work on a large or small scale? How much studio space do you have available? Do you prefer to work standing up or sitting down? You may in fact be quite happy to work at a table or with your drawing board or canvas balanced on your knees, in which case you won't need an easel at all. (My own easel languishes in a cupboard, hardly ever used. I paint mostly in watercolour and I prefer to work on a flat surface.)

To help you make your choice, here is a brief survey of the easel types available, along with their relative pros and cons.

Studio easels

A studio easel is ideal for artists who do a lot of large-scale paintings. The heaviest ones are extremely sturdy, standing firm even when you paint vigorously. The canvas or board rests on a ledge that also forms a compartment for paints and brushes, while a large sliding block holds it firmly in position at the top. Some models are on wheels so that they can be moved around the studio. They are all expensive to buy, take up a lot of space, and are not collapsible.

Radial easels

The rigid radial easel is very popular and provides a good, less expensive alternative to the studio easel. Sturdy and versatile, it consists of a central pillar with adjustable tripod struts. The central joint tilts back and forward at different angles, and the height is adjustable for sitting or standing. The canvas rests on a shelf with room for brushes, while the top locks into place with a sliding block. When not in use it can be folded for easy storage.

Artists' "donkeys"

If you prefer to work sitting down, the

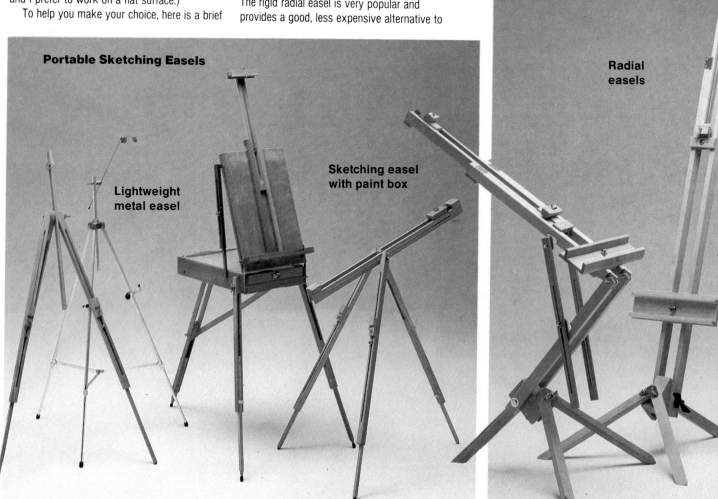

Portable Sketching Easels

Lightweight metal easel

Sketching easel with paint box

Studio Easels

Radial easels

traditional "donkey" provides both a seat and an easel in one convenient unit. The angle of the easel can be adjusted and the canvas or drawing board is held firm by a sliding block. Being fairly low off the ground, however, the "donkey" offers a restricted view of the subject and takes up a lot of space.

Table top easels

The table top easel provides a useful, compact support for smaller paintings and drawings and can be folded flat for storage when not in use. It consists of a frame to hold a drawing board, that is propped up on slats at the rear, giving a range of tilted angles. A good one will have pads on the bottom to prevent it from slipping. The board can be rested on the frame without being clamped, so is easy to remove and place

on a flat surface if desired. Aluminium easels are lightweight and inexpensive, but not very stable and are easily toppled over. Wooden ones are much sturdier.

Sketching easels

The tripod-style sketching easel is lightweight and easily portable, and is suitable both for sketching and for outdoor work. Available in aluminium and wood, it has adjustable legs to enable you to work at a convenient height and the pivoted central section can be tilted to a horizontal position for watercolour work.

The wooden box easel is sturdier than an ordinary sketching easel, but equally portable. It combines a collapsible easel with a wooden box for carrying painting equipment in one compact unit, and can be carried like a small suitcase. In use, the box folds down and forms a useful tabletop for holding paints and other equipment. Most models have telescopic legs that clip to

the side of the box, and can be adjusted to the desired height and angle for painting.

Drawing boards

The function of a drawing board is to provide a firm support for your drawing or painting surface. Commercial wooden boards sold in art supply stores are fine, but it's less costly to get a good piece of hardboard or fibreboard from a timber yard instead. They are lighter to handle and can be cut to fit your needs, but make sure they have a smooth surface as any roughness can transfer to the paper. Whatever size board you choose, it should be at least 2.5cm (1in) wider than the painting surface on all sides. This will encourage you to draw more freely, and also prevents the paper from buckling when the board is fitted onto the easel. If the drawing board feels too hard, put a few extra sheets of paper under the top one to create a more yielding surface.

Table Top Easels

Aluminium　　　**Wooden**

Artists' donkeys

TECHNIQUES

Renoir once observed that "painting isn't just day-dreaming, it is primarily a manual skill, and one has to be a good workman." This section deals with the "nuts and bolts" of painting and drawing portraits – the essential skills and techniques that will enable you to express, through your chosen medium, what you wish to communicate. It starts by explaining the principles of drawing the head in proportion and gives advice on how to draw and paint particular features such as the eyes, mouth, hands and hair, as well as on which colours to mix to achieve lifelike skin tones. It then discusses the various painting and drawing media, their suitability for portrait work, and specific techniques and methods associated with each one. By trying out different media, techniques and approaches, you will soon develop your ability and your confidence.

In this pastel portrait, Ken Paine used only two colours so as not to detract from the simplicity of the drawing. The emphasis is on shape, angle, line and balance.

DRAWING THE HEAD

Beginners often stress the facial features as the most important aspect of a portrait. But if the overall structure, proportions and planes of the head are correct, the features will fall naturally into place.

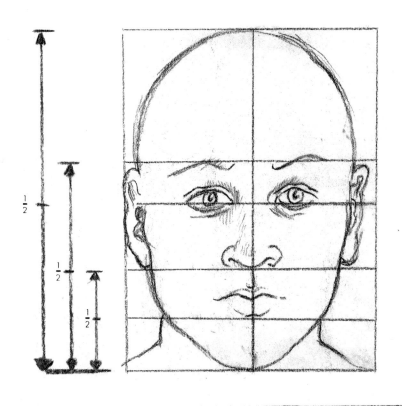

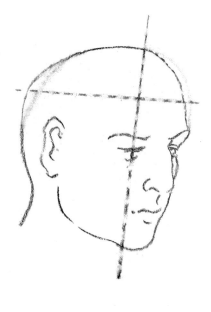

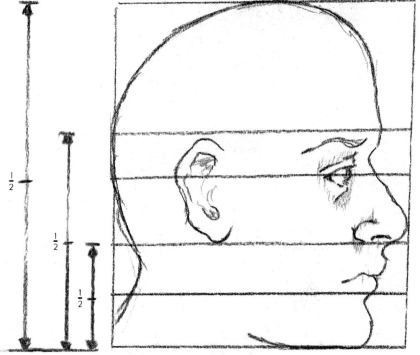

Above: To assess head proportions in a three-quarter view, use your pencil, held at arm's length, to compare the length of the head to the width.

Left, and above left: When drawing the human head it is essential to get the basic proportions correct. As a rule of thumb, the main features divide the face up into thirds (this applies both to front and profile views, as the two diagrams show). But remember that the proportions will vary from one individual to another.

When you first set out to draw a complex form such as the human head it can be difficult to know where to begin. As with any painting subject, it is easier to first visualize the head in terms of simple geometric shapes: thus the head and neck resemble an egg sitting on top of a cylinder. When viewed from the front the "egg" is upright and fits more or less into a rectangle. From the side the egg is tilted at an angle of roughly 45° and fits into a square.

Once you have established the shape and tilt of the head, you can position the features. Here you will find the "rule of halves" useful as a guideline. First divide the egg in half horizontally and then vertically. The vertical line acts as a guide for the position of the features on either side. The horizontal line marks the position of the eyes. Now divide the space between the top of the eyebrows and the bottom of the chin in half to find the position of the base of the nose. Finally, draw a line halfway between the nose line and the chin to establish the position of the lower lip. These measurements apply whether the head is viewed from the front or the side.

These "rules" of head proportion are based on the average person, who, of course, doesn't exist in real life. They are intended only as a guide, but they will enable you to see more easily the differences in proportion that distinguish one head from another.

Three-quarter view

When viewed from the front, the head is basically egg-shaped, appearing longer than it is wide. As it turns to one side, more of the back of the head is revealed and the distance from the forehead to the back of the skull becomes longer. As an aid to getting the head in correct proportion, use your pencil as a sighting tool to measure, say, the distance from the top of the head to the chin and compare it to the distance from the forehead to the back of the skull.

Correctly placing the features in a three-quarter turned head is a matter of careful observation and, again, the use of comparative measurements. The drawings here show how the centre line running between the eyes and down through the centre of the mouth moves closer to one side the further the head is turned away from view. Having sketched the basic head shape, it's a good idea to lightly draw in this centre line as it will help you to align the features correctly. The mouth, for example, is commonly drawn too far to one side; its centre should align with the base of the nose. The eyes, too, are commonly mis-aligned. Seen from the front, they are roughly one eye-width apart, but in a three-quarter view they appear slightly closer together. They also differ from each other in size and shape, the near eye appearing larger and more elongated.

Above: If you look at a head in profile, you will see that the nose, mouth and chin each recede slightly from the one above. The upper lip recedes from the tip of the nose, the lower lip is set back from the upper lip, and the chin recedes from the lower lip. This does of course vary from one individual to another, but the basic guideline holds true for the majority of faces.

Left: One of the hardest things, when the head is between front and side profiles, is to place the features correctly and in proportion. It helps if you locate the centre line of the face; its location will depend upon how far the head is turned.

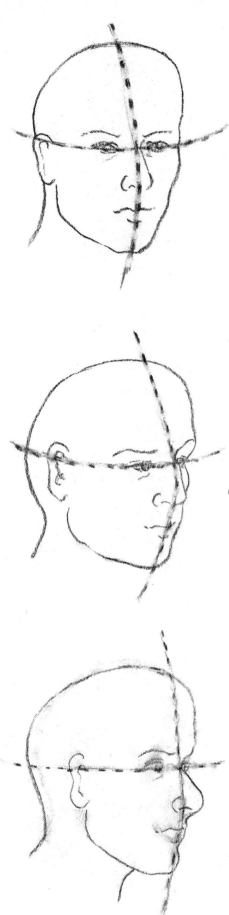

Profile view

In a profile view the contour line of the forehead, nose, mouth and chin is important in obtaining a good likeness of the sitter. Having sketched out the overall shape of the head and roughly positioned the features using the "rule of halves" (see page 33), you are ready to draw the features of the person in front of you. A good tip is to hold your pencil with a straight arm in front of you to align vertically with the tip of the model's nose and then to observe the shapes above and below the tip of the nose. These "negative" shapes, between the outline of the face and the straight line of your pencil, make it easier to judge the angle of the forehead and nose, and how far the chin juts out or recedes.

When the ear is visible, it will help you to place it correctly if you compare the distance from the corner of your model's eye to the back of his or her ear with the distance from the eye to the chin. They will be approximately equal.

An easy mistake is to place the eye either too close to the bridge of the nose or too far back. To check its position, compare the eye width with the distance from the front of the eye to the bridge of the nose.

Neck, arms and shoulders

The neck, arms and shoulders should be carefully studied as they are of obvious importance in half and full-length portraits.

Below: In this portrait by David Graham, the diagonals of the arms form a counterbalance to the pose and help to break up the space in the lower half of the picture in an interesting way.

When posing your model, aim for an attractive and harmonious arrangement — arms and hands hanging limply are death to any portrait. Think of the head, neck, shoulders, arms and hands as a series of interlocking parts, each connecting with and emerging from the other. For example, the shape of the shoulders is largely dependent on what the arms are doing, an upward or sideways tilt of the head must be accompanied by a corresponding tension in the neck, and so on.

Because forms are divisible by their names — neck, shoulder, arm, hand — beginners tend to draw each one separately and this is why the forms appear stiff, angular and wooden, like a series of broken sticks. Instead, try to see the underlying curve that flows from the head right down to the fingertips and follow its action with your pencil. Don't be timid — dive in straight away with a confident, sweeping line that follows the contour from the top of the head to the tips of the fingers. "Feel" the forms as you go, varying the pressure on your pencil to suggest the soft fleshiness of the upper arm and the hard angularity of the elbow.

Form and volume

When painting or drawing a portrait, it is important to first look at your subject as an arrangement of light and dark masses that convey a sense of form and volume. Beginners almost invariably make the mistake of first drawing an outline around the figure which is later "filled in". This is understandable — after all, it's the way we are all taught to draw from a very early age — but the result is that the subject looks more like a cardboard cut-out than a living, breathing person.

Watch any professional painter at work and you will see that instead of imposing lines and shapes *onto* the support, he allows them to emerge gradually *out* of it. It's rather like watching a photographic image taking shape in the developing tank: at first all you see are a few pale, blurred shapes, but gradually the image sharpens and becomes recognizable.

Have the courage to put down the masses of the face and figure as broadly as possible from the beginning. First lightly sketch in the proportions of the subject, then immediately model in tone the main light and dark masses, both of the subject and the background (it helps if you use a large brush, or a soft, responsive drawing medium such as charcoal or chalk). The edges and contours of the figure are not all cut and dried; the lighting conditions may cause some parts of the figure to appear to blend into the background, and much of the poetry of a drawing or painting is attained by softening an edge here and omitting a detail there, so as to leave something to the viewer's imagination.

By thinking first in terms of large masses, you will find you progress in a natural sequence from broad, sweeping strokes to smaller, more precise strokes, while maintaining the overall structure. In the sequence **above and right**, George J.D. Bruce first uses thin paint to lay in the main masses of light and dark. Working on all areas of the canvas at once, he builds up the lights, half-tones and shadows and ensures that they are correct in relation to one another. Only when the painting is near completion does he begin to sharpen up details and bring the picture into focus.

FACIAL FEATURES

Before you can paint a successful portrait you need to know how to draw individual features of the face and body. You will find no lack of models among your own family and friends, and you can catch them while they are reading, watching TV or snoozing in an armchair. You can also practise on yourself using a mirror.

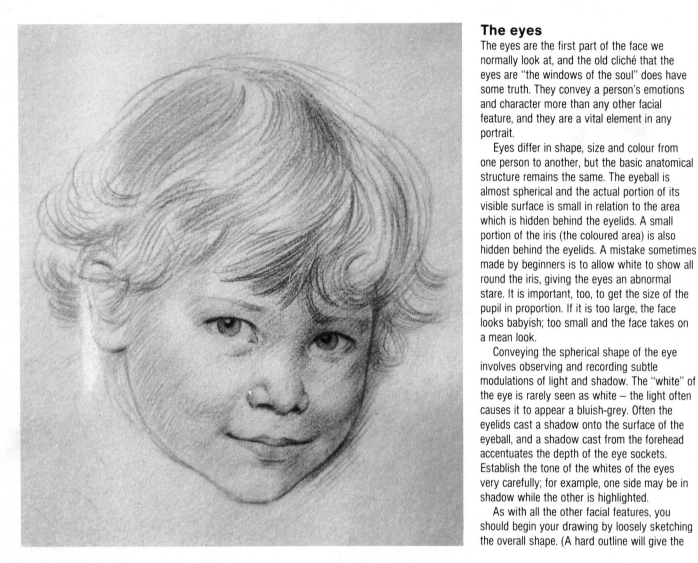

The eyes

The eyes are the first part of the face we normally look at, and the old cliché that the eyes are "the windows of the soul" does have some truth. They convey a person's emotions and character more than any other facial feature, and they are a vital element in any portrait.

Eyes differ in shape, size and colour from one person to another, but the basic anatomical structure remains the same. The eyeball is almost spherical and the actual portion of its visible surface is small in relation to the area which is hidden behind the eyelids. A small portion of the iris (the coloured area) is also hidden behind the eyelids. A mistake sometimes made by beginners is to allow white to show all round the iris, giving the eyes an abnormal stare. It is important, too, to get the size of the pupil in proportion. If it is too large, the face looks babyish; too small and the face takes on a mean look.

Conveying the spherical shape of the eye involves observing and recording subtle modulations of light and shadow. The "white" of the eye is rarely seen as white — the light often causes it to appear a bluish-grey. Often the eyelids cast a shadow onto the surface of the eyeball, and a shadow cast from the forehead accentuates the depth of the eye sockets. Establish the tone of the whites of the eyes very carefully; for example, one side may be in shadow while the other is highlighted.

As with all the other facial features, you should begin your drawing by loosely sketching the overall shape. (A hard outline will give the

Below: Some points to watch out for when drawing eyes.

Above: A child's eyes are larger in proportion to the head than those of an adult. They are also very expressive and appealing, as this drawing by John Edwards shows.

Wrong The iris is centred in the socket, giving a "staring" appearance.

Right The iris is partly covered by the eyelids.

Wrong Hard outlines give the eyes a flat, cartoon-like look.

Right Soft lines and shading give a more natural result.

Highlights are important in giving the eyes sparkle.

eyes a "pasted-on" look.) Then build up the form of the eye and the area surrounding it at the same time, so that they blend together naturally. You will notice that the shape of the eye comprises two semi-circles, the upper one being slightly more curved than the lower. A curving, irregular line will give an impression of the eyelashes – never attempt to paint individual eyelashes.

The sparkle that gives life to the eyes comes from the moisture on the rounded surface catching and reflecting light. Light also travels through the eye and illuminates the iris. To capture the sparkle of the eyes you must observe carefully the different tones and highlights. For example, the brightest highlight on the eye will sparkle more if the whites of the eyeballs are toned down slightly.

The mouth

The mouth is second only to the eyes in expressing an individual's character and mood. A complex of delicate muscles around the mouth make it capable of an infinite range of shapes and expressions, and it is this mobility which makes it one of the most difficult features to draw convincingly. The most common mistake is to draw the outline of the mouth first and then fill it in with colour, which gives it a flat, pasted-on appearance. In order to capture the roundness and soft, mobile appearance of the mouth it is best to avoid a rigid outline and model the shape with light and dark tones only. When the basic shape is correctly modelled, finish off by adding one or two crisp touches on the line between the lips.

The following general rules will help you to draw mouths accurately, so that you can concentrate on recording the exact likeness of a particular mouth.

The lips follow the shape of the jaw and the teeth behind, which curve outward. The upper lip is usually thinner and slightly darker in tone compared with the lower lip, which is fuller and

When the mouth smiles, the whole face smiles.

Lips do not rest on a flat surface but follow the shape of the jaws and teeth, which curve outward.

An open, smiling mouth has a narrowed upper lip. It is unusual to see the bottom teeth revealed.

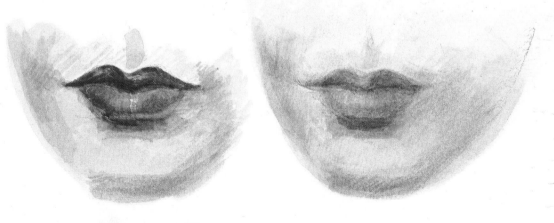

Right: Wrong The lips appear "stuck on" to the face; the outline is too hard, and the colour too red.
Far right: Right Soft outlines make the mouth appear mobile, and the colour is more natural.

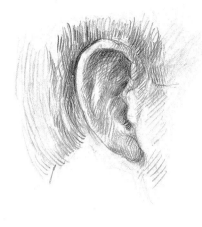

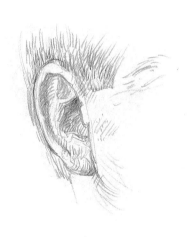

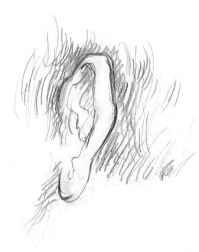

Above: This pencil portrait by John Edwards shows the position of the ear in relation to the size and proportions of the head. Notice how far back from the face it lies: people often make the mistake of placing the ear too far forward.

Left: The form of the ear may seem complex at first. Practise by drawing the ears of your friends while they chat or watch TV. Draw ears from several different angles, from full face round to back view, until you have a three-dimensional understanding of their structure.

softer, especially in women and children. The bottom lip is also slightly shorter than the top one, and lighter in tone because it catches more light.

Smiling lips become narrow and elongated, and the line separating the lips turns up very slightly at the corners. This throws the flesh above the corners of the mouth into shadow. A fully open smiling mouth has a narrowed upper lip and the upper teeth are visible. Observe carefully the tone of the teeth — most will be slightly in shadow, with one or two lighter highlights near the front. The shapes of the teeth are most effectively represented using light and shade, rather than drawing a line between each individual one.

Above: The basic form of the nose is a wedge-shaped mass. The top part is narrow and bony; the lower part is cartilage and flesh, and forms the central "bulb" between the two nostrils. It is useful to lightly sketch in the underlying wedge-block construction of the nose before building up the more subtle formations with shading.

Right If the nose is drawn in outline, instead of naturally from the frontal plane of the face, it appears flat and two-dimensional.

Far right: Here the form of the nose is modelled with hatched and crosshatched strokes of varying density. Shadows, mid-tones and highlights – not outlines – describe the form of the nose and the surrounding area.

Below right: Observe the highlight running down the bridge of the nose and above the nostril.

When using colour, don't make the mistake of painting the lips too red. Use the same colour mixtures used in the skin, with the addition of just a touch more red. Also beware of making the mouth too dark between the lips – it is seldom as dark as it appears.

The ears

Don't worry if you feel confused at first by the complex whorls and curves of the ear. By drawing individual ears from different viewpoints you will soon develop an eye for their relative size and their position on the head. The tricky part is getting them to look as if they are growing naturally out from the skull, and not glued on!

The nose

The nose definitely projects from the face, and it is all too easy to render it too flat by relying on line drawing to shape it rather than modelling its form with light and shade. You will normally find a dark shadow at the base of the nose, and a slightly lighter one down one side if the light is coming from the opposite side. Define the bridge of the nose with a highlight, and place a small dot of light at the tip. Pay attention also to the nostrils and "wings" of the nose, which are often drawn too small.

Hair

Many people are puzzled about how to paint or draw hair, the difficulty being how to describe

Top: In this sketch the hairline is too rigidly drawn, giving a hard, unnatural appearance.
Centre: This drawing is much better; by lightening the pressure on the pencil, the artist merges the hair naturally into the forehead. **Above:** Here, sensitive line work softens the outline of the hair and suggests the play of light.

Top right: In this self-portrait, Lucien Pissarro's rather splendid beard is painted with loose scumbles using dryish paint. Notice the variations in colour and tone within the beard, and how the artist softly blends its edges into the skin of the face and into the dark clothing.

with line and tone something which is comprised of many individual parts. Although we know that hair is not solid, it is easier to consider it so when painting and drawing. The most common error is in trying to render individual strands, using line alone, with the result that the hair resembles strands of spaghetti. The secret of rendering hair is to go for the overall shape and mass first, and then indicate the direction of growth with a few light strokes. Have a look at some portraits by Albrecht Dürer or Rembrandt, in which the hair looks extremely realistic, and you will see that it has first been established as a solid mass.

Sketch in the overall hair shape first, then note how the hair is subdivided into smaller shapes, either by its styling or by the play of light and shade, and indicate these shapes with

broad strokes. Having established the basic form, add some textural strokes in the same direction as the hair curls or falls. Finally, a few wisps and strands will complete the illusion and play off nicely against the more tonal areas. Always use a light, sensitive touch, making feathery strokes rather than pressing hard with the brush or pencil.

The direction in which the light falls on the head is important. For example, more light is reflected on top of the head if the model is lit from above. Think of the face and hair as a single form, not as two separate entities. If a shadow falls across the face, it falls across the hair as well, darkening its tone.

Another common error is to define too abruptly the area where the face and the hair meet, giving the sitter the appearance of

wearing a wig. To make the hairline more natural, lightly soften the edge where the face and hair meet and, if you're using colour, run some of the skin colour into the hairline. The same technique can also be applied to the outer contours of the hair, which can be blended subtly into the background. This will give an impression of the softness of the hair and create a feeling of air and light around the head.

The colour of the hair can also create problems, but bear in mind that it should look soft and natural. Like skin, hair is not one solid mass of colour, but a combination of light and dark tones which may be cool in the shadows and warm in the highlights: you will see subtle hints of blue and brown in black hair, blond and red in brown hair, and brown, gold and grey in blond hair. In addition, hair picks up and reflects colour from its surroundings, especially if it is shiny. Try to paint hair to harmonize with the skin colouring, using a similar palette as the basis for both sets of mixtures.

Above left: Ken Paine conveys the vitality of his subject by drawing rapidly and with great freedom, using both the side and the point of his pastel sticks. The black hair and beard are enlivened with blue highlights.
Above right: Paine uses the dramatic effect of strong highlights and deep shadows to capture the model's strength of character. In men, beards, moustaches and eyebrows are very important in identifying an individual; here the thick moustache is highlighted to give it emphasis.
Left: This is a portrait of two sisters, painted by George J.D. Bruce. The older one, on the left, has sleek blonde hair which reflects the light, while the other sister has an auburn mane of leonine hair.

HANDS

Many of us shy away from including hands in a portrait, convinced that they are too difficult to draw. But as hands frequently complement the composition of a portrait and are not as difficult to draw as they might appear, they are worth giving thought and practice to.

Even in a finished and detailed portrait, hands are often dealt with in quite sketchy and general terms and yet look very effective — often a few well-placed brushstrokes will suffice. If the hands are rendered in too much detail they distract attention from the face.

Hands are easier to draw if you begin by reducing them to their basic shapes and then fill in the planes of light and shadow. Try to think of the hands as complete structures of bone and muscle and resist the temptation to draw them piece by piece, with the fingers added one by one to the base.

Take every opportunity to draw individual hands — ask friends and family to keep their hands still for you while they are reading or watching TV. The hand is an extraordinary feat of human engineering, capable of a wide variety of movement and positions, and it is very expressive. You could fill a whole sketchbook with drawings of hands — broad and muscular, slender and graceful, gnarled and worn, hands outstretched or clenched, hands holding a cup or book, hands propping up chins — the possibilities are endless.

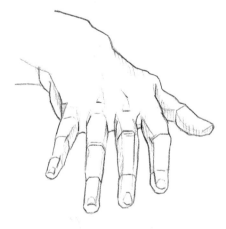

Left: The hand is used most expressively in this charcoal portrait by Zsuzsi Roboz. Note how the forefingers push up folds of skin at the temple, while the subject chews ruminatively on the lower fingers. This is clearly a study of a man deep in thought.

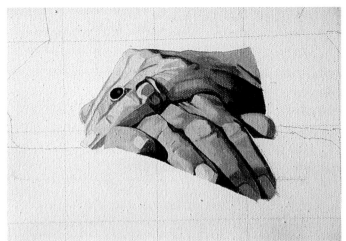

Above: In this detail from the portrait on page 87, the form of the hands is built up from three basic skin tones — light, medium and dark. The artist has observed carefully the lie of each finger in relation to the next.

Above: The form of the hands is expressed here simply and surely, while the slightly rough skin texture is suggested with rapid hatchings. William Bowyer has arranged the hands carefully so as to lead the eye in a circular path through the composition.

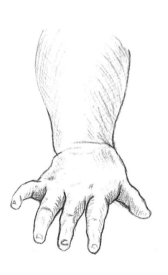

Far left: To simplify the process of drawing hands, it is helpful to begin by making a block sketch, in which each finger joint is treated as a rectangle. Then practise on your own hands, and different types of hands until you feel secure about the basic anatomy.

CAPTURING A LIKENESS

It is only when your portrait is completed that the moment of truth arrives.
Does your masterpiece actually resemble the sitter? Hopefully it does, but
even if you are not too happy about the likeness, don't be disheartened. What
is more important is a portrait that reflects an understanding of your subject
and an insight into their character – this makes all the difference between a
portrait that is merely competent and one that is convincing and alive.

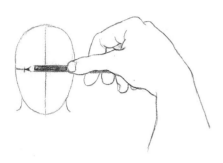

Achieving a likeness is partly a matter of
getting proportions right; it is about sound
drawing and close observation of the person,
coupled with an eye for detail. But, most
importantly, it is about capturing the *personality*
of the sitter. As we have already seen, the pose,
surroundings, lighting, and your choice of
brushstrokes or line handling can all say more
about a particular person than just an accurate
reproduction of the features.

Most beginners, in their eagerness to capture
a sitter's likeness, concentrate on the facial
features. These are of course important, but
other factors are equally important, such as the
shape of the head and its tilt, the set of the jaw,
and the general demeanour of the person.
Before you even put pencil to paper, step back
and absorb a general impression of your subject
and an overall sense of proportions. Is he or she
tall and erect, relaxed and languid, or hunched
and tense? This will need to be conveyed
through your drawing or brushwork. Check the
size of the head in relation to the torso, the
length of the arms, the width of the shoulders in

Right: Michael Noakes made
this pencil study of the late,
great actress, Dame Margaret
Rutherford, in preparation for an
oil portrait. Though it is a simple
drawing, we know exactly who
the subject is, because the artist
has conveyed the familiar twinkle
in Dame Margaret's eyes, her
knowing smile, and the
characteristic tilt of her head. In
some ways a portraitist has to
work almost like a cartoonist,
isolating the particular features
of the subject that most directly
reveal their personality.

Left: Part of capturing a likeness
is getting the features in correct
relation to each other. Use your
pencil as a measuring tool to
gauge relative distances and
relationships between points of
importance. For example, where
does the corner of the eye lie in
relation to the corner of the
mouth? How does the width of
the head compare to the length?

relation to the head, and so on.

Work *from the general to the particular*. Look first for the dominant angles, masses and shapes, sketch out the framework, and only then start to refine the drawing with smaller details. This process of reduction allows you to see the head, or the figure, as a whole and not just a collection of separate parts. After all, a sculptor doesn't take a chunk of marble and carefully chip out a nose here, an eye there. He works with large planes and masses and once he's got these right he can then get down to the finer details.

When considering proportions, look and look again, mentally checking one feature in relation to another and checking angles and distances.

Look also for any distinguishing features that are unique to your sitter. Is the forehead receding or protruding? Is the jawline strong or weak? Are the eyes large, hooded, widely spaced or close together? In most faces, the eyes fall midway between the top of the head and the bottom of the chin, but check the specific head before you. When a likeness is off, it is often because there is something wrong with the mouth. Check the width of the mouth in relation to the width of the head, and the size of the upper lip compared to the lower. By constantly measuring and comparing in this way, you will find that every feature will emerge correct since it is correct as to size and position in relation to all the other features.

Above: Good likenesses are the result of capturing the personality of the sitter, not just their superficial physical appearance. In this drawing of HRH The Prince of Wales, Michael Noakes portrays the thoughtful, sensitive side of the Prince's nature. The eyes, directed to a point outside our vision, help create an aura of reflective introspection.

If all this sounds a rather dry and mechanical way of approaching a portrait, remember that with practice and experience it will become instinctive.

USING COLOUR – FLESH TONES

What colour is skin? There is no definitive answer to this question because human skin contains an infinite variety of hues, and its overall colour depends on such factors as race, age, sex, general health and degree of exposure to the sun. In addition, the reflective surface of the skin picks up light and colour from its surroundings.

To create lifelike flesh tones, you must discard all preconceived notions about skin being "white", "brown" or whatever. "White" (Caucasian) skin is not always the pink and rosy thing some assume it to be, but ranges from pale ivory to olive to red and ruddy, with every shade in between.

It is possible to buy tubes and sticks of colour for portrait painting labelled "flesh tint", a pinkish colour which is supposed to resemble the colour of skin. These are best avoided; they make the skin appear over-pink, flat and lifeless, like that of a plastic doll. It is better by far to mix your own colours, as this gives you a much wider range of tints and shades with which to capture the subtlety and translucency of human skin.

The basic paint mixture for white skin comprises of various proportions of the three primary colours – red, yellow and blue. A good basic flesh tone can be obtained by mixing together roughly equal quantities of white (except in watercolour), yellow ochre and light red, plus cobalt blue for the shadow areas. Reds, umbers, siennas and greens can also be added to obtain the exact hue required. By adjusting the proportions of these colours you can create a range of light and dark, warm and cool flesh tones with which to model the planes and volumes of the face and figure, and to evoke the play of light and shade on the surface of the skin.

With coloured races there is a very wide range of skin tones, from pale gold to rich brown to ebony. Avoid using too much black in

Above: In this *alla prima* oil painting, Anthony Morris sees many hues in the subject's flesh tones, from warm pinks to pale ochres and grey-greens.

Right: The artist's palette consisted mainly of alizarin crimson, oxide of chromium and white, plus chrome yellow in the warm areas.

Left: This model's skin ranged from quite ruddy in some places to almost translucent white in others. In his pastel portrait, Barry Atherton has carefully observed the changing colour temperatures across the surface of the skin.

Below: The artist used several colours, in a wide range of tints, including gold ochre, madder and purple brown, brown-grey, raw umber and white.

your flesh mixtures, because, no matter how dark-skinned your sitter is, solid black simply goes "dead". Dark umbers, siennas, violets, greens, oranges and blues, mixed together in varying proportions, provide rich, deep tones that capture the sheen of the skin.

Analyse closely the colour of shadows and highlights on the skin – they are not just a darkened or lightened version of the basic flesh colour but contain their own colours, which are often affected by the reflections of surrounding colours. You will notice, for example, how skin looks lighter and warmer on its rounded, light-struck areas than it does in receding or shadowed parts. The forehead, nose, cheeks and chin will probably contain warm reds and yellows, while eye sockets, the area under the chin, and the shadow side of the nose may contain cool blues, and green-greys. Such colours may seem surprising in the context of what we normally think of as "flesh" colour, but if you look hard enough you will see them. Renoir did, and he is renowned for the vibrancy of his skin tones.

The way in which flesh colours are mixed together can also help to give the impression of the skin's texture. In oil and watercolour, for example, thin transparent glazes of colour can be built up, allowing the white ground to show through and lend a certain luminosity to skin tones. Small, separate strokes and dabs of

Right: The white of the paper plays a vital role in this watercolour study, creating an impression of strong light shining on the model's face. Lucy Willis has rendered the skin with a combination of glazes and wet-in-wet washes; the resulting portrait has a fresh, lifelike quality that is special to the watercolour medium.

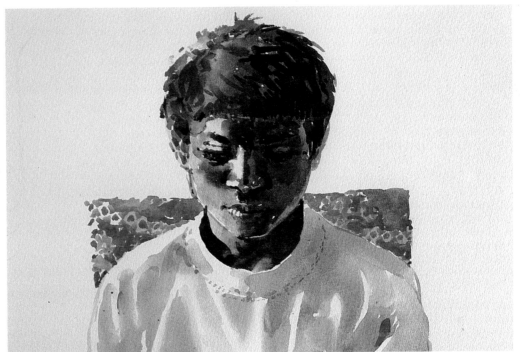

Above left: The artist used a basis of cadmium red and yellow, cobalt blue and violet in various proportions, with cerulean blue, Paynes grey and alizarin violet in the cool areas.

colour, in the Impressionist manner, suggest the play of light on the skin, and this method is particularly appropriate when drawing with pastels and chalks. These and other techniques are discussed more fully on pages 58–59.

OIL PAINTING

Over the centuries, oil paint has been the favourite medium of portrait painters. The smooth, buttery consistency of oils, coupled with their slow drying time, means that they can be manipulated freely and extensively on the support to produce an infinite variety of textures and effects – a distinct advantage when modelling the complex forms of the human face and figure.

There are two basic approaches to painting in oils. First, there is the traditional approach, in which thin layers of colour are built up slowly and in a considered way, often on top of a carefully planned underpainting. Then there is the direct *alla prima* approach, in which the painting is usually completed in a single session and without any underdrawing or underpainting.

The method you adopt will depend partly on the personality and mood you wish to convey in the portrait, and it is likely that you will find yourself adopting elements of both approaches in the same painting. There are few rules in oil painting, and much can be left to your own imagination and insight. One principle that should be observed, however, is that of working "fat over lean". Most oil paintings are built up of several layers of pigment and if eventual cracking of the paint surface is to be avoided it is important that the initial layers consist of "lean" paint (paint mixed with more turpentine and less oil). The use of oil in the mixing medium should be increased as the layers of paint are built up. The reason for this is simple: if "lean" paint is applied over "fat" (paint mixed with a higher percentage of oil than turpentine) the lean layer dries first. Then, as the fat layer underneath begins to dry and contract, it will cause the dry paint on top to crack.

Toned grounds

Once a canvas or board has been primed it can be given a wash of colour using thinned paint applied with a rag or brush. A toned ground serves two purposes. First, it softens the stark white of the canvas or board, which can make it difficult to assess colour and tone accurately. Second, if the succeeding colours are applied patchily the ground will show through and become an integral element of the painting, helping to unify the colour scheme and tie the painting together.

The selection of the colour for the ground will be determined by your subject. It may be a neutral grey or earth tone, or it may be chosen to provide a contrast to the overall colour scheme. For example, a cool undertone of soft green such as *terre verte* will have a vitalizing effect on the warmth of the skin tones in a portrait.

To make the wash, dilute the paint wih turpentine to a very thin consistency and apply it with a large brush or a rag. An oil ground usually takes 24 hours to dry thoroughly, but if time is short you can use acrylic paint for the ground and overpaint in oils.

Monochrome underpainting

The idea of an underpainting is to block in the main shapes, masses and tones of the composition with thin paint in a neutral colour, prior to the application of glazes and layers of opaque paint. The basic principle is to give you an idea of what the final picture will look like before you begin the painting proper. Composition, the distribution of light and shade, drawing and proportion – all of these elements can be checked, and any alterations made quite easily at this stage. The result is a practical division of labour: once the underpainting is complete you can begin working in colour, confident that the composition and tonal values are correct. This is the time-honoured method of working in oils, which was used by Rembrandt, Rubens and many other great masters.

Choose a neutral colour for underpainting, such as raw umber, *terre verte* or grey and, following the principle of "fat over lean", dilute the paint with turpentine to a thin consistency. Use a large brush and block in the main shapes and masses only: as the underpainting will eventually be obliterated, there is no point in putting in too much detail.

Far right: This portrait by Richard Foster has a gentle, timeless beauty. Sitter and background are fused together by the cool, silvery light, conveying a moment of tranquility. The use of oil paint has enabled the artist to achieve an overall softness.

Glazing Here a dilute glaze of yellow has been laid over a dry underlayer of blue. The two colours combine optically – in the viewer's eye – and take on a resonance impossible to achieve by mixing them physically on the palette.

Scumbling is another method of optical mixing. The idea is to paint a semi-transparent layer, like a haze of smoke, over another colour which has already dried. The paint can be worked with a circular motion, or in various directions, leaving the brushmarks showing. Here, blues, pinks, and yellows were scumbled together with short, scrubby strokes.

Glazing

Glazing is a method of laying thin washes of heavily diluted paint one over another so that each layer modifies the one beneath. Glazes, being transparent, allow light to pass through them and reflect back off the canvas. This gives the colours a unique depth, glow and richness unobtainable by mixing them physically on the palette. Glazes can be applied directly over a light underpainting or, alternatively, after the thick, opaque paint layers have been applied. Shadow areas in particular appear more luminous when deepened with a dark glaze.

For a glaze, dilute the paint to a thin, but oily consistency and apply with a large, soft-haired brush. Glazing is a slow process as oil paint takes a long time to dry and each layer must be fully dry before the next is applied. Nowadays, special glazing mediums are available, which dry relatively quickly and impart a soft lustre to the paint surface.

Scumbling

A scumble consists of short, scrubby strokes of thin, dry, semi-opaque colour, applied loosely over a dry underlayer. Because the colour is applied unevenly, the underlayer is only partially covered and shimmers up through the scumble; the interaction between the two layers creates a soft, pearly effect while retaining the liveliness of the paint surface. Small amounts of scumbled colour can be effective in modifying an existing one. For example, try a light scumble over a dark colour, a cool scumble over a warm colour, and vice versa. Scumbles also tone down and unify passages that are too "jumpy".

Using a flat, stiff brush (either bristle or nylon), a rag, your fingers or the edge of your hand, lightly scrub the paint on with free, vigorous movements in various directions. The aim is to paint a semi-transparent overlayer like a haze of smoke.

Impasto

When colour is applied thickly to the support with a brush or knife it is called impasto. This may be applied to certain areas of the picture to emphasize form and texture or to accentuate highlights; or alternatively the whole surface can be impastoed to give a rich-textured effect. The paint is mixed up on the palette and applied generously with a well-loaded brush or knife using rapid, vigorous strokes. In his later paintings, van Gogh worked in this way, often squeezing the paint straight from the tube and "sculpting" it into swirling lines and strokes.

Wet into wet

This is a fast, direct method of applying colour, and is often used in *alla prima* painting. The colours are applied over or into each other while

Below: In this striking portrait, Anthony Morris applied the paint rapidly in the *alla prima* manner, juxtaposing broken patches of warm and cool colour, blended in places, to describe the planes of the face in a bold, uncompromising way.
Impasto right: Oils, thick paint and rapid brushstrokes can be built up to create a lively and energetic surface.

MORRIS

they are still wet, leaving them partially mixed on the support.

The soft, pliant nature of oil paints allows for a considerable amount of wet in wet blending. By slurring the wet colours together you can achieve subtle gradations of tone and colour, so essential when modelling the rounded forms of the face and figure. Beware of overworking the brushstrokes, however, as this takes the life out of the colours, and allow some of the brush marks to show for more lively effects.

Broken colour

The term broken colour means the application of small strokes or dabs of colour side by side or overlapping each other, but without blending them together. This is known as optical mixing, and from the normal viewing distance the separate strokes of colour appear to merge and the forms become more distinguishable. But because the strokes are fragmented they reflect more light and so appear more luminous than blended colour.

This technique is usually associated with the French Impressionist painters, who showed that by applying paint, not in flat areas but in small, separate strokes, they could convey a stronger sense of light and movement.

The paint should be fairly thick and dry so that each brushstroke retains its shape.

Right: In this oil sketch of her daughter, Lucy Willis builds up the forms with rapid strokes applied directly to a canvas tinted with a warm undertone.

Wet-in-wet, above: is a technique often used in oil painting, where each stroke is painted next to or over another wet stroke to produce lively colour mixtures and softly blended forms.

Broken colour, right: Small strokes of pure pigment, applied without blending, build up to create a mosaic of shimmering colour.

Right: Ian Sidaway demonstrates the use of a mahl stick (see page 17). The stick is used to steady the hand when tackling detailed areas of a painting.

WATERCOLOUR

Watercolour is an excellent medium for spontaneous, informal portrait studies. Its inherent qualities of translucency and fluidity are perfectly matched to the subject: soft washes bring out the bloom of the skin and capture the play of light on the face and figure, while crisp lines and strokes provide texture and detail.

Above: Ian Sidaway has used delicate washes and glazes to create a subtle and lifelike portrait.

Above right: Watercolour is the perfect medium for capturing the sparkle of outdoor light. Portrait by Lucy Willis.

Because watercolour is transparent, paintings are always built up from light to dark, beginning with the white of the paper and applying successive layers of colour, called washes, until the desired tones and colours have been established. The lightest areas are represented, not by adding white paint, but by leaving patches of white paper bare.

Washes are the foundation of watercolour painting. You can have a lot of fun practising the various types of wash, and the time will be well spent. Watercolour is an unpredicatable medium and only experience will tell you how much paint and water will be needed to create a smooth, transparent wash with no marks or runs. A good tip is to work on damp paper so that your colours can flow together naturally. This also makes it easier to lift out colour for highlights or to wipe out mistakes.

Don't be afraid to "splash out" when applying washes, as working in a dry and sparing manner results in a lifeless painting. Mix more paint than you think you'll need and apply the colour with a large, well-loaded brush. Keep your wrist supple and work quickly, confidently and broadly so that the brushstrokes flow into each other. Once a wash is applied, leave it to dry undisturbed.

Graded wash

A *flat wash* is one that is even in strength. In a *graded wash* the colour moves gradually from dark to light, or light to dark. The method of application is the same as for a flat wash, but with each successive stroke the brush carries more water and less pigment, or vice versa. Graded washes are useful in describing the soft, rounded contours of the human form, and also for creating tonal interest in a plain background.

In *wet in wet* painting, a wash is laid on damp paper and, while it is still wet, another wash is laid next to it or on top of it. The colour bleeds into the first wash and partially mixes with it, creating a soft, hazy effect. This is an exciting technique because the results are unpredictable. The trick is to allow the first layer to dry just a little before adding another so that they blend without running out of control. By tilting the board in the appropriate direction, you can also control the direction and flow of the paint. It is best to use a heavy grade paper, stretched and firmly taped to the board, as then

Below: Susan Ryder harnessed the immediacy and spontaneity of watercolour to create this lively portrait of her father. The paint is applied with dash and bravura, leaving areas of bare paper to serve as highlights. In the shadow area of the face, the artist lifted off some of the colour with a tissue as it dried, giving a marvellous impression of reflected light.

Wet-over-dry Washes of transparent colour can be built up, like layers of tissue paper, to obtain a wide range of colours and tones.

Left: The freshness and delicacy of watercolour is well suited to the portrayal of children. In this portrait, *William Smallbone*, Sally Hope employs selective focus, painting the child with more colour and detail and gradually "fading out" the details of the background.

Below: In this portrait of a fisherman, William Lee Hankey employs the traditional watercolour techniques — wet-in-wet, wet-on-dry and drybrush — to build up a richly textured surface. Observe how a range of cool blues and blue-greys has been partially mixed, wet-in-wet, to breathe air and life into the area behind the figure. Using hard edges in some places and softer, more blurred edges in others keeps the figure from looking as though it has been stuck onto the background.

Drybrush A very distinctive, lively texture can be achieved by dipping an almost-dry brush in paint and dragging it lightly over the surface of the paper.

it doesn't buckle when wet washes are applied. The technique of wet in wet is useful for painting backgrounds, as the soft, indistinct shapes produced give an impression of space.

In the *drybrush* technique, a small amount of pigment is picked up on an almost-dry brush and skimmed lightly over a dry surface. The paint catches on the raised "tooth" of the paper, leaving tiny speckles of the paper, or the underlying colour, showing through. The ragged, broken quality of a drybrush stroke is effective in subtly describing the texture of, for example, hair. The technique works best on a medium- or rough-textured paper.

The transparency of watercolour means that washes of two different colours can be laid on top of one another to create a third colour. For example, a wash of yellow followed by a wash of blue will give you a delicate, transparent green. Allow each paint layer to dry before applying the next, otherwise the colours will mix together and turn muddy. If you try to do this with more than two or three colours the transparency of the colour will be lost because the white of the paper will be obliterated.

You cannot add a light colour over a dark one in watercolour, so you must first decide where the lightest areas are and then paint around them. It helps to plan your watercolour before starting to paint, and a light outline drawing in pencil is a useful guide for laying washes. I would stress the word guide here — don't fall into the trap of filling in rigid outlines in the "paint-by-numbers" style so that each area of colour is separate and distinct; the

essence of watercolour is spontaneity, and sometimes "happy accidents" occur which add a little poetry to the painting.

Painting around small or fiddly white shapes – say the highlights on the eyes and lips – can be a problem because they interrupt the "flow" of the surrounding wash as it is applied. An effective answer is to paint over the areas to be preserved with masking fluid. This liquid, rubbery solution is applied with a brush and dries almost instantly to form a paint-resistant film that enables a wash to be applied on top of it. When the painting is dry the mask is removed by gently rubbing with the finger, revealing the untouched paper below.

Masking fluid creates bright, precise, hard-edged highlights. For softer highlights, gently lift out some of the colour from a damp wash using a clean, soft brush, a tissue or a piece of blotting paper.

Below: Ian Sidaway's technique is precise and highly graphic. The artist squints up his eyes to simplify the tones in his subject, decides which areas to leave white for highlights, and then applies his colours with clean, crisp washes.

Right: Jacqueline Rizvi works here on tinted watercolour paper and adds touches of white body colour to her pigments in the light areas. Her colours are built up gradually with small strokes and dabs, to achieve a mosaic of colour and tone that seems to vibrate with light.

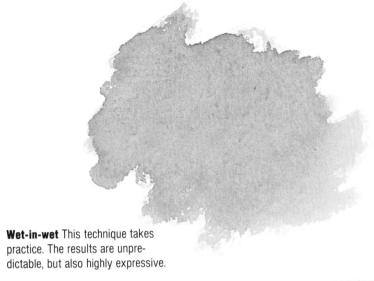

Wet-in-wet This technique takes practice. The results are unpredictable, but also highly expressive.

CHARCOAL AND PENCIL

Pencil and charcoal are so immediate and responsive in use, they are almost like an extension of the artist's fingers. They give a full tonal range and also a sensitive line, enabling you to convey a sense of light and life in your portrait drawings.

Charcoal

Charcoal is a uniquely expressive medium with a delightful "feel" to it as it glides across the paper. With only a slight variation in pressure on the stick you can produce a wide range of effects, combining strong and vigorous linear work with soft smudges.

Because charcoal blends and smudges so easily and possesses rich tonal qualities, it is an ideal medium for *sfumato* drawing. The Italian word *sfumato* means "softened" or "evaporated", and in drawing the term refers to the use of very subtle tonal gradations to describe objects without drawing outlines or contour lines. This can be achieved either by rubbing the charcoal into the paper with the fingers so that the forms dissolve together, or by applying a dense layer of charcoal and picking out the lighter tones with a kneaded or putty eraser.

Pencil

The character of a pencil line is influenced by the grade of pencil used, the pressure applied, the speed with which the line is drawn, and the type of paper used. Hard pencils make fine, incisive lines and are really only appropriate for fine work. Soft pencils are more appropriate for portrait work as they give more varied lines and tones and can be used on their side to produce solid areas of tone. Pencils glide easily over a

Above: In this powerful drawing by Zsuzsi Roboz, the charcoal lines were washed over with water to dissolve and spread the particles and produce the subtle tones.

Above: Ian Sidaway developed the subtle contours of the boy's head in areas of delicate shading, using extremely fine hatched strokes with a hard pencil. Areas of untouched paper indicate the highlights on skin and hair.

Charcoal makes a wide range of expressive marks. Rubbing with a finger creates a smooth tonal gradation from delicate grey to deep, rich black (**top**). Or try snapping off a small piece of charcoal and applying side strokes on textured paper (**above**). This gives an interesting broken effect. **Left:** Hatching and crosshatching in pencil. By increasing the density of the lines a range of tones can be obtained.

Hatching

Crosshatching

smooth paper and give clean, unbroken lines; on a rough paper the bumps "catch" the pencil mark, giving broken lines and tones.

Several grades of pencil can be used in one drawing and can result in a rich diversity of tones and lines bringing out the textural qualities of hair and skin, creating the illusion of solid form and the play of light on the face.

Light and dark tones are achieved by varying the pressure on the pencil or by varying the space between hatched or crosshatched strokes (see page 60), and a tonal area can be "drawn" into with a putty eraser to create highlights. Working in pencil allows for as much elaboration and reworking as you like; in fact, some artists prefer not to rub out their mistakes and re-workings, as these exploratory lines can add life and spontaneity to the finished drawing.

These two drawings demonstrate the versatility of charcoal. In the larger study Susan Ryder emphasizes the strong contrast between the sitter's dark dress and her pale skin. In the smaller study, the girl was dressed in white, in a sunlit room, so the tones were closer and more subtle.

PASTEL AND CRAYONS

Superb portraits have been done in pastel, crayon, chalk and pencil. These media have the advantage of directness and great speed – there are no colours to be pre-mixed, no drying times to worry about, no brushes or palettes to clean. In short, there is nothing to get in the way of your direct response to the subject.

Right: This pastel portrait by Ken Paine vividly demonstrates the strength and vigour of pastel. The artist uses broken strokes of colour throughout and leaves some areas of the painting rough and unfinished. The overall impression is one of tension and pathos.

Pastels, chalks and crayons are extremely versatile in that they can be both a drawing and a painting medium. By simply twisting and turning the sticks, using the tips and the sides, you can create a wide range of effects, from vigorous lines to broad "washes" of colour. For this reason pastels and crayons are equally appropriate for finished, detailed portraits and for rapid drawings and preparatory sketches. Coloured pencils are slightly less flexible because, with the exception of watercolour pencils, you can't blend the strokes so easily. On the other hand, coloured pencil work has a uniquely crisp, fresh, graphic quality.

With a drawn, as opposed to painted portrait, some areas of the paper are usually left untouched, showing between the lines and strokes as well as around the borders of the subject. There are many paper colours to choose from, and you will find that a well selected paper contributes much to the overall effect of the finished work, helping to tie the picture together and to enhance the colours of the subject.

The texture of the paper is important, too. If your style is bold and vigorous, a rough paper will give better results because its uneven texture is capable of holding more pigment. Also its rough surface breaks up the colour and

Above: In *Portrait of a Painter*, Barry Atherton employs a free, bravura style that lends verve and sparkle to the portrait. In places he builds up the pastel thickly, in others he uses feathering and broken strokes to animate the picture surface.

produces more expressive lines. Smooth-textured papers, on the other hand, are better for fine detail and linear work as well as softer, more even blending.

Mixing colours

"True" painting media – oils, watercolour, etc – can be mixed on a palette to the colour you want and then applied to the working surface. But pastels, chalks and pencils cannot be pre-mixed; instead the colours are mixed on the paper surface itself. This can be done either by *physically* blending and layering different colours together using your fingers, a brush, rag or *torchon*, or by allowing them to mix *optically* – in the viewer's eye. Optical mixing means applying small, separate strokes of pure colour without blending, so that the picture is built up

Soft blending

Partial blending

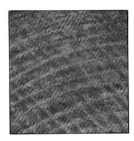

rather like a mosaic. From a normal viewing distance these strokes appear to merge into one mass of colour, but because they are fragmented the colours "flicker" on the eye and appear more luminous than a solid area of blended colour. This technique is particularly effective for capturing a sense of light and animation.

You can get a good feel for the possibilities of drawing with colour by making practice "doodles". The examples here show a variety of strokes and marks that can be made, each of which will breathe life and energy into your portraits and figure studies.

Blending

Soft pastels and chalks, being powdery, can be blended very easily to create a wide range of subtle textures and effects. Colours and tones, either adjacent or on top of each other, can be softly fused together by gently rubbing with your fingertip, a rag, a paper tissue, a soft brush or a *torchon*. Sharp lines can be softened, shapes

tied together, tones lightened or darkened, and forms modelled from light to dark.

Hatching and crosshatching

These drawing techniques – a form of optical blending – have been used for centuries as a means of building up areas of tone, colour and texture using line alone. In hatching the lines run parallel to one another; in crosshatching they cross each other at an angle. Simply by varying the density of the strokes, it is possible to create a wide range of tones; closely spaced lines create a dark tone, widely spaced lines a lighter tone. By interweaving strokes of different colours it is possible to achieve hues of great subtlety and complexity. This is particularly effective for depicting skin tones, where many reflected colours are found in the highlight and shadow areas. Finally, the lines themselves convey energy and movement, particularly when they run in different directions, following the contours of the subject being drawn and describing its form and volume.

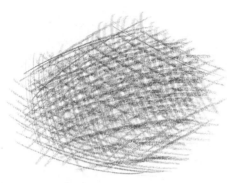

Above: These are examples of multiple crosshatchings in pastel (*top*) and coloured pencil (*bottom*). Vertical and horizontal lines were laid in and then crosshatched with diagonal strokes. Subtle and intricate colour harmonies can be obtained by interweaving strokes of different colours.

Right: Madeleine David uses vigorous strokes, hatched and crosshatched, to lend strength and authority to this coloured pencil portrait. Some of the strokes follow the contours of the face; elsewhere the strokes run this way and that, overlapping and creating colour rhythms and tensions. The underlying surface is used freely as a cool accent tone on the forehead, nose and cheeks.

Scumbling

Feathering

Scumbling

Neither mixing colours nor rectifying mistakes are as straightforward with pastels, chalks and crayons as in other media. Once a colour has been laid down, it cannot successfully be erased, and adding another colour on top can lead to a clogged and tired-looking surface. Scumbling is therefore an invaluable technique because it allows you to modify colours that you are not happy with. Use the tip of the stick and apply very light pressure to make loose, scribbled strokes creating a thin veil of colour that doesn't entirely cover the one underneath. Don't overdo it or the underlying colour will be completely obscured. The two colours will mix optically (in the viewer's eye) and have a pleasing vibrancy which is often lacking an in an area of flat, blended colour.

Feathering

Like scumbling, feathering is a useful technique for enlivening an area of colour that has gone "dead", or for modifying a colour that is too dark, too light, too warm, or too cool. For example, if you have rendered an area of a cheek too pink, you can tone down the colour by feathering over it with strokes of its complementary colour — green. The underlying colour is still apparent, but is modified by the feathered strokes. Feathered strokes can also be used to soften an over-defined line, or to blur the division between light and shadow. To feather one colour over another, use a hard pastel or pastel pencil to make light, feathery strokes in a diagonal direction over the area to be modified.

Above: Lucy Willis has applied the pastel very freely, with large areas of the brown paper left uncovered to provide a unifying middle tone.

Right: Here, Julia Midgley has combined watercolour wash, pastel and pastel pencil to create a range of delicate textures. Bold shapes and a simple colour scheme give the portrait a graphic, poster-like quality.

APPROACHING
THE SUBJECT

Painting people requires not only an understanding of the construction of the human form, but also the ability to interpret and express the character and mood of the subject. A pleasing portrait is one which, apart from its purely aesthetic appeal, also leaves us feeling that we know the sitter. Many professional portrait painters often spend as much time planning the picture as they do making it, because every aspect of the image – the sitter's pose and clothing, the background, lighting, colour scheme and composition – has a part to play in expressing the individuality of the sitter. This section takes you through all the stages of planning a portrait, and you will also find many kinds of portrait approached in different ways: male and female, children, the elderly, double and group portraits, self-portraits, outdoor portraits and informal portraits.

By practising on family and friends you will soon be able to express your own artistic style.

The Pianist *by Wilfrid Gabriel de Glehn, RA (1870–1951),*
100 × 76cm (40 × 30in). Oil on canvas.

KEEPING A SKETCHBOOK

Carry a sketchbook and pencil with you as often as you can, and try to sketch every day. There is no better way to improve your drawing skills and your powers of observation, and through time you will build up a visual diary which can be fascinating to look back on.

Your sketchbook is your most valuable piece of "equipment". It is the perfect place in which to practise skills and techniques, to develop new ideas, and to work out problems of colour, composition and tone. It's also a place to note and record anything of interest, and as such becomes a valuable storehouse of visual references which can be used later on in your paintings. A sketchbook also helps to build up your confidence; rapid and frequent sketching helps you to express more intuitively what you feel and see, and any initial stiffness in your drawing will soon disappear.

Even if you are out at work all day, there are bound to be moments when it is possible to make a few drawings of people: sitting on a train, or in a café at lunchtime, perhaps. A sketchbook is easily hand held, so you can work discreetly without attracting attention – a distinct advantage when sketching people, who can become very self-conscious when they perceive they are being sketched. Try not to use an eraser too much; after all, a sketch is a *working drawing*, so don't be afraid to let your mistakes show.

Above: The play of light on the face is the emphasis in this sketch by Zsuzsi Roboz.

Right: This rapid pen sketch speaks volumes about the character and mood of the subject.

Above: Drawing people unawares requires a responsive medium that will perform quickly and expressively. Stephen Crowther used pen and ink for this sketch of his mother and father.

One joy of sketching children is that they don't have the self-consciousness of adult subjects. This naturalness offers scope for touching and memorable studies.

COMPOSING THE PORTRAIT

The term composition applies in many of the arts. In music it refers to the arrangement of notes and rhythms that produce a complete, harmonious piece. In the visual arts, composition means the intentional distribution of forms, shapes, colours and tones to produce a unified whole.

Composition is an important element in any painting. Even a simple head-and-shoulders portrait against a plain background needs to be composed so that the subject fits effectively within the confines of the picture space. Before you embark upon your painting, you need to step back and evaluate your subject, not only as a living person occupying three-dimensional space, but also as a flat pattern – a "jigsaw" of interlocking shapes, colours and tones – that adds up to a balanced design. There are certain fundamental questions you should ask yourself, about where to position the subject on the paper or canvas, how much space to leave around the subject, where the focal point of the picture will be, and about how to create rhythms and tensions that steer the eye through the picture.

Backgrounds
Backgrounds play a supporting role in most portraits, but they still require some thought and attention. The background setting should be planned carefully as an integral part of the portrait, implying something about the subject's character by its colour, tone, and any specific details it might contain.

When deciding on the composition of a portrait, remember that the background is part of the "jigsaw" of shapes, tones and colours that make up the whole picture. Are the "negative" shapes around and behind the "positive" shape of the subject interesting and varied? Are there any jarring lines or rhythms that might spoil the balance of the composition or compete with the main subject? Look out for obvious "false attachments" such as horizontal

lines that cut across the middle of the picture and verticals that appear to sprout from the model's head.

A well-planned background should establish a sense of balance in the composition and maintain the focus of attention on the sitter. For example, if you have placed the sitter off-centre, you may wish to position an object in the background to counterbalance this shape. Also, the colours and tones in the background can be used to complement those of the model's hair, complexion and clothes. For example, cool colours in the background will emphasize the warm tones of the skin; dark clothing and hair are generally more effective against a light background, and vice versa. It is a good idea to keep a collection of drapes and backcloths so that you can try out various options. When in

Above: A diagram showing the position of the four "intersections of thirds". Locating your centres of interest at or near these points helps to produce a well-balanced composition.

Left: In this portrait by Richard Foster, the placing of the head – to which the eye is immediately drawn – is balanced by the position of the hand at the bottom left of the picture. Both lie close to points roughly one third of the way in from either side of the canvas.

Squaring up

When working out the composition of a portrait, you will probably make a small pencil or charcoal sketch, or a monochrome sketch in paint to serve as a "trial run" for the finished painting. However, many people experience some difficulty in translating a small sketch into a large image. "Squaring up" is the easiest way to do this accurately, and is demonstrated here by artist George J.D. Bruce. This technique, also known as "scaling up", involves drawing a grid of equal squares over the sketch. A larger version of the same grid is then drawn on the support to be painted, and the image transferred square by square to obtain an accurate enlargement. For example, if you are doubling the

size of your sketch, each square will have to be twice the size of the grid square on the sketch.

In his original oil sketch **top**, the artist used a time-honoured method which can be seen in preparatory cartoons from the Renaissance. Here, before committing the composition to the large canvas, he made a

monochrome sketch in thin paint to work out exactly how the figures would relate to each other. Then he drew a grid of squares over the image. Ensuring first that the proportions of the larger canvas were the same as those of the sketch, he then drew the same number of squares, only proportionately larger, onto the canvas. (Always use charcoal or thin paint when drawing onto canvas, as pencil is apt to show through all but the thickest paint.) The forms on each square could now be drawn onto their corresponding squares on the canvas so that both the details and proportions of the sketch were accurately transferred, before going on to complete the painting.

Above: *Symphony in White No. III* (1867) is a delightful example of James Abbot McNeill Whistler's famous series of "musical" titles – *Symphony, Arrangement* and *Nocturne* – where his emphasis lay in the harmonics of tone, colour and line. His portraits reveal his dedication to formal pictorial values in their composition, in the balancing of the poses of his models, and his sensitive use of colour.

Left: The artist can select the format best suited to the composition by using two L-shaped pieces of card and moving them to extend or shorten the edges. After making sketches of her model, Susan Ryder decided on a horizontal format for the final painting. The upright format didn't work here because the vertical of the model's right leg was too insistent. The horizontal format gives a more balanced result, with plenty of space on either side of the model.

doubt, choose a neutral colour or a middle tone for the background, against which the lights and darks in the portrait will be clearly defined.

If you choose a plain background, grade the colour from light to dark, or include the sitter's shadow to suggest the space between the figure and the background. If you were to paint it as a flat colour, your portrait would look as if it were pasted on.

Balance and proportion

Although good composition quickly becomes intuitive as you gain experience, there are certain guidelines that will help you at the outset. For example, it is best to avoid placing the figure too close to the edge of the picture, or cutting the sitter's arms off at the wrists, both of which create a discordant, uncomfortable feeling. As a general rule, try to place the head so that the space on the side toward which the head is turned is just a little greater than the space behind; if the space on either side of the head is equal the effect is static and symmetrical.

It is useful to have a pair of L-shaped cardboard pieces with which to "frame" your intended subject. By sliding the L's together or apart you can alter the size of the aperture and

create a square, horizontal or vertical format, and explore the various compositional options.

The traditional way to produce a balanced, satisfying composition is to apply the "rule of thirds". This formula is based on mathematical principles of harmony and proportion, and has been used by artists for centuries. Mentally divide your paper or canvas into thirds, horizontally and vertically, and locate points of interest at or near the points where the lines cross. In a head-and-shoulders portrait, for example, the eyes are normally the focal point. To give them maximum impact, and to position them in a balanced and pleasing way, you may wish to position the head so that the eyes are about one third of the way in from either side of the canvas.

The rule of thirds can also help to position secondary elements such as the hands, or objects in the background. This simple principle produces well balanced, comfortable compositions that are easy on the eye – but you should take care not to apply it rigidly to every picture or you will soon find the results boring and repetitive.

Of course, the so-called "rules" of composition are not inviolate, and they are regularly broken by experienced artists.

THE POSE

The human body is capable of an infinite range of movement, and therefore the choice of pose for a portrait is also infinite. Moreover, with each new sitter you'll encounter a different personality, and half the fun of portrait painting lies in deciding how best to bring this out: pose, expression and surroundings can all contribute to the final effect.

Right: The sitter's pose often helps to underline the mood of a portrait; here the pose is a contemplative one. Compositionally, the upward diagonal of the arm is important because it counterbalances the downward slant of the head, creating an interesting visual tension. Charcoal drawing by Zsuzsi Roboz.

The word "pose" is somewhat misleading. It suggests a forced, artificial position, whereas the most important factor in posing is to get the sitter to look relaxed and natural. If the sitter is in a position that's uncomfortable, this will be reflected in your painting.

The sitter may feel a little awkward or self-conscious and will usually ask "how do you want me?" Simply ask him or her to relax and move around freely, and they will instinctively take up a pose which is both comfortable and expressive of their personality. We all express our character through "body language", and an outgoing, assertive person will use different expressions and gestures to a shy person.

Encourage conversation while you are working as this helps to bring a natural and animated expression to the face. Allow plenty of rest breaks during a sitting — every 15 or 20 minutes if the pose is a tiring one, once an hour if the pose is a more comfortable one.

In choosing a pose, there are many variables. Do you want the model standing or sitting, and

Right: Sometimes you don't need to pose your model at all — you can paint them while they're reading, watching TV, listening to music, or having forty winks. In this pastel study, Lucy Willis was interested in the way the light, coming from the window behind, outlined the contours of the sleeping figure. Notice also that the model's arms create an interesting shape, forming a circular path that leads the eye to the face.

Left: The subject of this painting is a physicist, and a world authority on geology and earthquakes. Zsuzsi Roboz has painted him in an appropriate pose, poring thoughtfully over a large globe of the world.

Below: Entitled *Musing*, this beautifully rendered painting by Norman Hepple expresses a strong sense of rhythm and design and demonstrates the importance of the sitter's pose to the composition of the picture. The eye is first drawn to the face, and from there the sinuous S-curve formed by the sitter's arms leads us down through the painting. The vertical on the left prevents the eye from moving out of the picture and directs us up toward the face again.

do you intend to focus on the face alone, or to include the whole or part of the body? Even in a simple head-and-shoulders portrait, an interesting pose is vital. A full-face or profile view is the most straightforward, but potentially rather dull and static. A three-quarter view, though less easy to draw, gives a greater range of expression, as does a head which is inclined or upturned slightly. A seated or standing pose offers you the chance to explore the possibilities of including background, props and clothing, thereby extending the expressive qualities of the portrait. In general a seated pose is more comfortable for the model and offers more possibilities — upright, reclining, leaning to one side, head propped on hand, and so on. A standing pose looks more formal and is more demanding of the model's stamina.

With a sitting figure, it is best to avoid a position which involves much foreshortening of the body and limbs, at least in the beginning. Be careful also not to cut the hands or feet off at the edge of the picture. The eye is directed to this cut-off point and the edge of the picture becomes unduly important, thus spoiling the balance of the composition.

It is often a good idea to include the sitter's hands (or just one hand) in the portrait. The hands are one of the most expressive parts of the body, and can give life and vitality to a portrait as well as playing an important part in the composition. Whether lying in repose in the model's lap, or engaged in some activity, they provide a secondary focal point. Echoing the tones of the face, they attract the eye and should be placed carefully so as to form visual "stepping stones" that guide the observer's eye through the picture and toward the face.

LIGHTING

When setting up your portrait, you should pay particular attention to the lighting. Whether you plan to use natural daylight or artificial light, remember that the purpose is to bring out the roundness of the head and the modelling of the features. The amount, direction and intensity of the light will also have a direct influence on the mood and emphasis of the portrait.

Three-quarter light brings out the sculpted planes of the head and gives a strong impression of form.

Side light is more dramatic, casting one side of the face in shadow.

With a backlight the head is cast in soft shadow, with a sliver of light illuminating the hair.

Left: In this watercolour portrait David Hutter captures the alert, open expression on the little girl's face, and the freshness and delicacy of her skin. Light falls on the sitter from in front, but her face is turned to one side, so that the light catches the side of her cheek and nose while the rest of the face is in soft shadow.

Portraits are more frequently painted indoors than outside, giving you the choice of natural or artificial light, or both. In general, natural light from a nearby window is best because it doesn't distort tones or colours. Traditionally, artists have favoured light coming from the north, because it remains consistent throughout the day and doesn't cast harsh shadows on the sitter's face. East, west, and sometimes south light are affected by the movement of the sun, so shadows will move as you are painting. In these cases, it is best to complete the painting over several sittings, each at the same time of day.

Though artificial light tends to distort colours and tones, it does have the advantage in that its strength and position do not change. Special "daylight" bulbs are available but, if a stronger light is required to provide distinctive shadows and modelling, a powerful tungsten bulb can be used.

A simple lighting plan is best, preferably a single source of light illuminating the subject from above. This lends solidity to the form and simplifies the tonal values. If the head is illuminated from two or more directions the lights, halftones and shadows are less easily distinguished, and drawing the roundness of the head and modelling features becomes more difficult.

Lighting sets the mood of a portrait, so before you begin painting, decide what mood and characteristics you wish to emphasize in your sitter and arrange the lighting accordingly. Do you want a soft or a striking effect? Are you more interested in emphasizing the physical features of the subject, or in revealing intimate aspects of his or her personality, inner mood and feelings? Even if you don't have a proper studio, it shouldn't be too difficult to create a particular lighting effect, using table lamps, spotlights or a window. Some of the most common lighting situations used in portraits, and their effects, are covered here.

Three-quarter light This is the type of lighting most often used for portraits. It is the most flattering and gives a strong impression of volume and surface texture. If your subject has a strong personality, use three-quarter light to help express their vigour and vitality. The light

Right: In a portrait of his wife, Ian Sidaway exploits strong directional light for this bold composition. The sunlight throws one side of the model into light, the other into shadow. This contrast is emphasized with crisp edges and the use of a very dark background.

source should be positioned above and slightly to one side of the sitter so that light illuminates about three-quarters of the face, with the rest in shadow.

Diffused light Diffused light is the light that falls all around us, such as sunlight filtering through clouds, or pouring into a room through a skylight or a large window. It is a soft light with no violent contrasts, and produces large highlights and soft shadows. Diffused lighting emphasizes qualities of delicacy and tenderness and has been used by portrait painters through the centuries, especially when painting women and children. To create this effect, place the sitter directly facing a low window so that the head is fully illuminated.

Side light When the face is lit from one side only, leaving the other side in complete shadow, the strong tonal contrast creates a sense of drama and tension. Check which side of the sitter's face is most flattered by the bright illumination, then seat him or her side-on next to a window or eye-level light source. If you feel the shadow side of the face is too dark, try placing a reflective board next to the sitter on that side to bounce some light back into the shadow. A large sheet of white paper taped to a board should do the trick.

Backlight Backlighting is not often used in portrait painting because it is not descriptive of the facial features in the same way as three-quarter light. However, if you want to capture a gentle, lyrical mood — in a portrait of a young woman, or a mother and child, for example — then backlighting can be very effective. When the sitter is positioned in front of a soft, diffuse light source such as a window, light coming from behind creates a luminous "halo" tracing the contours of the subject and lighting up the hair. The face, in contrast, is softly shadowed. The overall effect is soft and subdued, creating an air of quiet stillness.

Rembrandt lighting To recreate so-called Rembrandt lighting — named after the artist, who used it in many of his paintings — a small, concentrated light source is positioned high above the sitter so that light falls on him or her at a sharp angle. This creates a dramatic "spotlight" effect in which specific details — perhaps the top of the face and a hand — are picked out and the rest of the features are plunged into shadow. The mood generated can be enigmatic and mysterious, sombre or dramatic, as in Ken Paine's portrait on page 75. If misused, however, Rembrandt lighting can look stagey and theatrical. Be sure that you are using it for a purpose, and not merely as a facile mannerism.

Place your sitter beneath a high window, or rig up a spotlight on a high shelf so that the light falls on the subject at a sharp angle.

Above: Three-quarter lighting is popular with portrait painters who wish to emphasize the structure and character of their subject. This painting is by Sally Hope.
Below: For this portrait of a gardener, Stephen Crowther placed his subject against the main source of light, outdoors, while the weaker light indoors softly illuminates the features.

Above: In this quickly executed sketch Ken Paine conveys character and mood with a simplicity of effort. It is loosely drawn, leaving out detail — even the light areas speak for themselves.
Right: Paine's emphasis here was on the *chiaroscuro* effect of Rembrandt lighting. The dark areas balance the picture from bottom left to top right.

CLOTHING

The clothes that a sitter wears for his or her portrait should both reflect his or her personality and be in tune with the overall mood of the painting. If the face is to be the focal point of the picture, garments in quiet colours and restrained patterns are preferable; bright colours and strong patterns will compete for attention with the face.

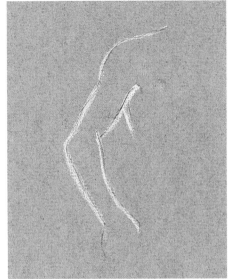

You and your sitter should agree beforehand about which clothes he or she will wear for the portrait. Some may want to wear a favourite sweater, or a garment which they consider flatterning. You, the artist, will be looking at the garment in terms of tone, colour, texture and overall shape, and how these will relate to the face and to the background.

In the majority of portraits the face is the focal point, and the clothing should be a part of the whole image and not allowed to dominate the pictue unless that is your specific intention. Any pattern in the clothing is best simplified so as not to compete with the face for attention. Don't attempt a precise, meticulous study of the pattern – suggest it with a few bold strokes rather than laboriously copying the design. It is important, however, to convey the folds and creases in the clothing, and the play of light and shade, which give the impression of the underlying form of the figure.

Drawing and painting folds and creases in fabric, especially if it is patterned, may seem daunting at first, but it becomes simpler if approached in a logical way. Look at the fabric, then divide it into portions according to the main folds and areas of light and shade. Notice how the pattern runs in different directions within each section.

It is a good idea to practise drawing folds by draping a piece of cloth over a simple object. Observe how the shape of the object determines the way the fabric falls; having noted how sharp creases give way to soft folds, and how light and shade creates form, you can then indicate these with subtle gradations of tone.

Above: When drawing folds in a garment, for example the creases in a sleeve where the arm is bent, it helps to lightly sketch in the relevant part of the body first and then outline the fabric folds over the top.

Above, left: The subject of this painting wanted to be painted in her wedding dress, which pleased the artist, George J.D. Bruce, because it gave him the opportunity to exploit the nuances of light and shade on the rich fabric. The highlights were built up with a thick impasto, which physically catches the light.

Left: Edwin Greenman has faithfully reproduced the texture and pattern of the old lady's knitted shawl, yet it does not compete with the face for attention.

INFORMAL PORTRAITS

For beginners especially, painting people can be an inhibiting task. But you don't *always* have to go for the formal portrait, perfectly composed. To gain confidence and develop your skills, why not start by painting informal portraits of family and friends?

Informal portraits are the artistic equivalent of a snap-shot, in which the subject is dressed casually and adopts a relaxed and natural pose, and the composition is similarly uncontrived. They can be great fun to paint and the result, if successful, is a lively image that captures the personality of the sitter more readily than a formal portrait might.

The informal approach is particularly effective with people who feel and look ill-at-ease if posing formally. If they are doing something they enjoy – a musician practising an instrument, a child playing with a toy, an aunt knitting – he or she will appear more relaxed and animated. And with the sitter

happily occupied, you, the artist, can work at your own pace, without feeling under pressure to get the portrait finished quickly before the sitter becomes bored and fidgety.

Think, too, about how you can include objects or special effects around the person to reveal more about them and to build up a more interesting picture. Painting people in their own environment puts them at ease and gives you an opportunity to reflect something of their personality and lifestyle in the background. An interesting development of this idea is to portray someone in an out-of-the-ordinary or unexpected way. For example, often people have hobbies or interests which allow them to

be shown in a new light and reveal another side to their character. For me, a good example of this was seeing a portrait of an eminent university professor I knew: instead of opting for the usual formal, stern-faced pose, the artist portrayed the professor relaxing at home in an armchair, wearing his beloved baggy corduroy trousers and an old sweater, happily absorbed in reading a book. This relaxed and intimate portrait revealed far more about the professor as a person than a formal portrait would have done. And of course, for the onlooker the inherent fascination of glimpsing "the man behind the mask" gives an extra dimension to the picture.

Opposite: In *Summer Dreaming* by Daphne Todd, the relaxed poses and pale-colour harmony of the painting underscore the mood of gentle reverie.

Left: Engrossed in his playing, the subject was relaxed and unselfconscious in the presence of the artist, Zsuzsi Roboz, who was able to capture the concentration on the musician's face, and the sensitive pose of his hands.

Below: In *Morning News*, Sally Strand conveys the easy familiarity of a couple relaxing with the newspapers after breakfast, he engrossed in his reading, she momentarily distracted by something outside the picture.

PORTRAITS OF WOMEN

A woman's face, perhaps more than a man's, is often expected to reflect many moods and emotions. From the enigmatic Mona Lisa onwards, there have been countless portraits of women and girls, in which the artist has sought to capture something of the "feminine mystique" that he feels lies behind the outer, physical shell of the person.

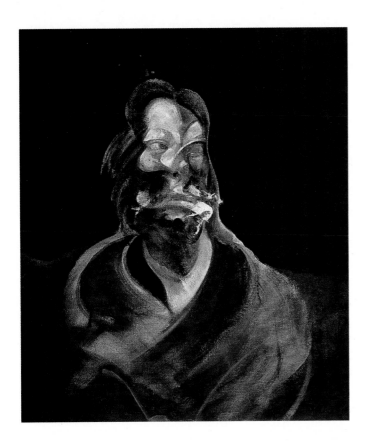

Left: Francis Bacon, who erupted into the international artworld in the 1950s, invented a new grammar of imagery in his portraits which identifies less with the sex or personality of his models than with figurative representation of 20th-century violence, fear and mental anguish. In this *Portrait of Isabel Rawsthorne* (1966) her features are dissolved and distorted by the dynamic brushwork, and the posture and line of the drapery proclaim an almost unbearable but compelling tension.

Opposite: In this delightful, informal portrait, Susan Ryder painted her daughter perched on the arm of a chair as if glancing up momentarily from her book. Rapid brushwork and light, high-key colours accentuate the air of youthfulness and vitality.

Below: Marian Carrigan's portrait of *Rachel*, on the other hand, is a bold, unfussy, instantly recognizable painting of a close friend. Executed in less than two hours in luminous, washy, fluid oils straight on to primed paper, the artist has captured the athletic physique, the femininity and the love of bright colour – the firm shoulder line, the flimsy camisole, the blue silk and the slash of lipstick – in this spontaneous, characterful portrait.

The general tendency in the past was to paint female subjects in a higher key and a lighter, less formal mood than male subjects; these days, most artists try to avoid such generalizations and treat the person on an individual basis. Before you begin the portrait, try to have a clear idea in your mind of the sitter's personality and her mood, and how she expresses these through her facial expressions, and her gestures and mannerisms.

An important factor is the age of your sitter. Obviously a young adolescent will project a different personality to a mature woman or a venerable old lady. Secondly, what *kind* of person is she? Confident and self-assured, or shy and retiring? A professional career woman, or earth-mother type? Is she calm and serene, or bouncy and energetic? Lastly, has your sitter requested a formal or an informal portrait? Each of these factors should be borne in mind when you come to decide on the pose, dress, composition, lighting, and the overall tones and colours of the portrait.

Assessing personality will present few problems if your sitter is someone you know well. But even if she isn't, you will find that most people convey something of their personality as soon as they enter a room. So be alert and watchful, looking out for any "giveaway" gestures or mannerisms. Try to draw the sitter into conversation about her work, her interests, her family, anything that will reveal something of the inner person.

This portrait was a private commission, painted in the setting of the model's own home. The artist, Susan Ryder, spends a great deal of time ensuring that background details are in keeping with the personality and mood of the sitter. "I try to find a room in the house in which my sitter feels happy and which also has good light. It's important, too, that the subject's clothing links in with the overall style of the room: here, Alice's blue sweater harmonizes with the colours of the room, while her white skirt provides a tonal contrast. I made three preliminary sketches in charcoal, in which I refined and altered the composition and tonal arrangement. In the final painting, however, I changed the position of the cat so that it leans out against the sitter, creating a counterbalance to the overall verticality of her pose."

PORTRAITS OF MEN

With male portraits, many of the factors to be considered are the same as those for female portraits. There are, however, obvious differences that require a male portrait to be approached in a different way to those of women and children.

Left: When painting commissioned portraits, Susan Ryder often asks her sitters to bring a favourite chair with them to the studio, because she finds that it helps them to feel more relaxed and at ease in otherwise unfamiliar surroundings. This man seemed relaxed with his arms folded, so he was painted that way. Ryder also experiments with different lighting arrangements, aiming to find one that is flattering to the face and figure and which underlines the sitter's personality. This portrait was painted by electric light, which cast a warm glow onto the face. Notice how the dark, shadowy background is loosely painted, creating a sense of space and atmosphere around the figure.

Traditionally, portraits of men have projected a more sombre mood than female portraits. The colour key is generally lower, the backgrounds darker, the lighting more dramatic and the shadows stronger – all factors that contribute to a "masculine" aura of strength and dynamism. This stereotype is a product of our cultural heritage, and is far less rigidly applied these days than it was in the past, but it is still quite often seen in male portraits.

In general, a man's face and body are anatomically characterized by harder, more acute lines than a woman's. The most obvious differences are broader shoulders, a thicker neck, stronger jawline, wider, thinner mouth, a harder line to the forehead, more deeply set eyes and a deeper recess beneath the lower lip. Lighting becomes particularly important, because the pronounced facial planes and rugged features of the male will be better emphasized through high contrasts of tone. Three-quarter light, side light and Rembrandt lighting (see pages 72 and 74) are all suitable as they accentuate strongly modelled features.

As with any portrait, mood and the expression of personality require as much attention as the physical features. The way your subject dresses, speaks, gesticulates, and the attitude he adopts when sitting, all give important clues to his personality, which should be expressed through the physical form of the pose. If he has a strong, outgoing personality, you might ask him to lean forward, looking the viewer straight in the eye. If he is a shy, sensitive type, this can be expressed by a more passive pose and averted gaze. Men often feel more self-conscious than women about the idea of "posing", and will feel more at ease if they are portrayed doing something connected with their work or leisure interests.

Left: A good portrait often says something, not only about the sitter but also about the relationship between sitter and painter. In this portrait of her father, Naomi Wright uses colour, composition and pose to express a thoughtful mood which conveys the love and respect she feels for him.

Above: The subject of this portrait looked very athletic, but the artist perceived in him a sensitive inner nature. Zsuzsi Roboz has tried to convey this dichotomy in her drawing, particularly in the expression in the eyes.

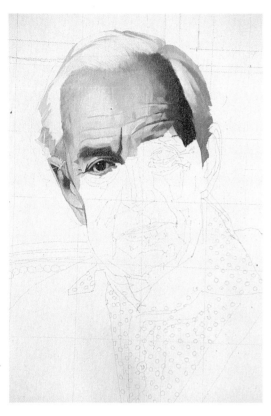

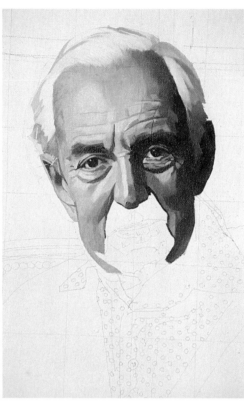

Ian Sidaway's early training as a graphic artist is reflected, to some extent, in his approach to painting portraits. Unlike many painters, he does not begin by estabishing the main masses of the image, working over the whole painting and adjusting the work as it progresses. He prefers to work systematically, starting in one place and filling in the image patch by patch, rather like a jigsaw puzzle. Many artists would find it difficult to work in this way, and the less experienced would be advised to bring the tones up together in relation to each other, his commentary on the six stages of the painting was . . .

"I made a careful outline drawing of the face with a well-sharpened pencil, indicating the areas of light and shade. I then started to paint the upper

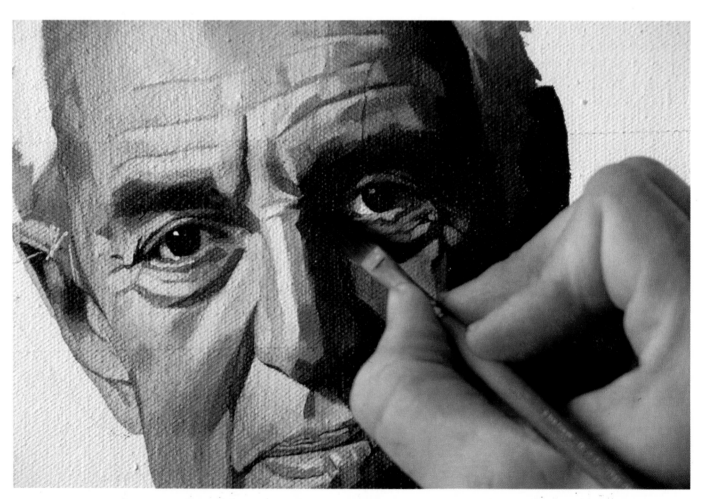

head and the eyes.

"I continued working down the face, carefully painting each area of tone or colour correctly in relation to its neighbour. By working from the top down, I avoided smudging the wet paint. The basic mixture I used for the skin tones was burnt sienna, cadmium red, cadmium yellow and titanium white, darkened with cobalt blue and ivory black in the shadows and in the folds of the

skin, and lightened with white plus a hint of yellow or orange in the highlights. I developed each feature in some detail and worked back to blend each new colour into some of those already established. The slow-drying quality of oil paint enabled these to be blended together to give the impression of soft, rounded form.

"I used a flat $\frac{1}{4}$-in (50mm) brush for most of the work because it gives me the clean,

sharp strokes I require.

"Having completed the figure, I then worked on the background. The reference for the Mediterranean-style windows was a postcard from the Greek Islands.

"I decided that the two windows in the background were too intrusive, and fought with the sitter for attention. So I painted out the window directly behind the figure.

"In the finished painting the

figure is accentuated by the stark white background. I added the pot of geraniums because they were in keeping with the sitter's surroundings and they added a contrasting colour accent. The geraniums also acted as a compositional device, tying the figure to the corner and balancing it with the window and shutter on the other side. As a final touch, I added a hint of texture to the wall using a graphite stick."

CHILDREN

Children have a universal appeal and make a particularly rewarding subject for the portrait painter. They are less self-conscious and react more spontaneously and naturally than adults, and their clear eyes, smooth skin and shining hair are a delight to paint.

Young children quickly become bored and fidgety if asked to pose for long periods, so the less formality involved in painting them the better. Rather than ask the child to adopt a formal pose, you will often get more interesting results by simply seizing an opportunity to paint as it arises – such as when he or she is sleeping! Children absorbed in some activity, such as playing in the garden, will be more likely to adopt a pose that is both natural and characteristic, and the end result will be a lively portrait that expresses the personality of the child as well as a good likeness. Similarly, while reading or watching television the child remains still but the face is mobile and expressive.

If you do choose a more formal portrait, think of ways to make posing fun and find something to interest the particular child. Play some music, tell a story, or carry on a conversation to put your subject at ease. Choose a simple pose that can be worked on over a period of time and pace the work to allow for frequent rests.

Opposite: Jane Bond painted young Tristan along with some of his favourite toys. The huge cane chair provides an interesting backdrop and accentuates the child's small size. The soft, dewy quality of young skin is captured beautifully here, using softly blended, but vigorous, strokes.

Below left: Sally Hope made this watercolour painting of Ben and Dougal while they were absorbed in the exploits of their favourite cartoon character. She has captured their look of intense concentration, a wonderful childish attribute that deserts us as we grow older and more cynical.

Below right: In this pastel portrait, *Biafran Boy*, Ken Paine concentrated on the shape of the head and the mobility of the child's expression. His approach was spontaneous and loose – he finds that, with children, the first impression is usually the most successful.

A fairly soft light that casts minimal shadows works best for children's portraits. Indoors, natural daylight from a nearby window will accentate the softness of a child's features. Out of doors, choose a position in open shade. It is best to avoid direct sunlight, as strong shadows will obscure details and expressions.

With patience and flexibility, it is possible to draw and paint even the most energetic or restless child from life. The secret is speed and practice. Before embarking on a full portrait, make frequent sketches of the child so that your pace of drawing is increased and you become familiar with the gestures and expressions used most often. These, and photographs too if you like, will provide valuable reference material when creating the actual portrait and adding the finishing touches.

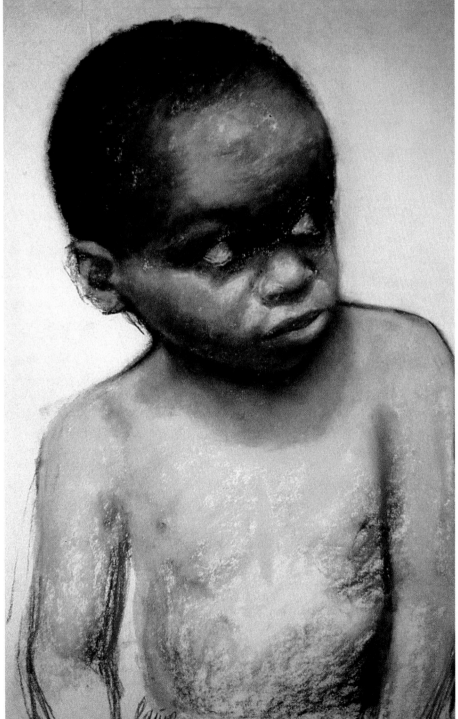

Charm and the innocence of childhood are the theme of this oil painting by Susan Ryder. Since young children are not always the most patient of models, the artist had to work quickly to capture personality, mood and, of course, a good likeness.

"In 1984 I was chosen by Pears Soaps to paint a portrait of that year's "Miss Pears". They wanted a very large picture, but the child was very small, so my first problem was a compositional one. I turned the situation to advantage by placing the figure of the child in the centre of the canvas and allowing the surrounding space to accentuate her small size and qualities of innocence and vulnerability. At the same time, I needed something to break up the monotony of the background, and I hit upon the idea of painting the child sitting on the floor, cutting out her own newspaper cuttings of the "Miss Pears" competition. As well as giving the model something to do, it also enabled me to use the patterns of light and shadow on the paper as a device to lead the eye to the figure of the girl. The cuttings, being relevant to the theme of the painting, also added an extra element of interest, while not being so obtrusive as to distract attention from the main subject.

"When painting children's portraits I avoid doing too many preliminary drawings, otherwise the child becomes bored before the painting has even begun. I settled for one watercolour sketch (**above**) to establish the composition and the colour values. I decided on an overall blue tone and a dark background, which would enhance the child's pale skin and hair, and the white of her dress."

PORTRAITS OF OLDER PEOPLE

Capturing the experience and character reflected in the faces of older people is a marvellous challenge for the portrait painter. Such aspects as lighting and the pose of the sitter enhance the mood conveyed by the picture and make the portrait more convincing.

Below: Her Royal Highness Princess Alice was in her nineties when she sat for this portrait by Michael Noakes. The last surviving grandchild of Queen Victoria, she was a gracious, regal lady, as expressed here by her upright posture and the delicately positioned hands.

It is significant that some of the greatest portraits ever painted were of elderly men and women. Look at the paintings of da Vinci, Velázques, Rembrandt, and many others, and you will find among them powerful and moving portraits that capture both the dignity and the vulnerability of old age. In many ways older people are more interesting to paint than pretty adolescents, whose faces are as yet unmarked

by experience. The lines and creases in a well-worn face reflect the joys and sorrows of a lifetime, and present the artist with an excellent subject for the study of character, mood and expression.

In most cases, you will be painting the portrait of a relative or a friend, someone who is well known and well loved, so you will be familiar with their habitual expressions the way

Left: Edwin Greenman painted this portrait of his mother when she was 96. She was a dignified, indomitable lady, and the artist tried to express this through a strong, triangular composition in which the sitter is placed slightly above eye level.

Right: Ken Paine enjoyed working on this portrait. He used energetic lines and bright colours for a lively effect, in keeping with the character of this sprightly old man.

they sit, fold their hands in their lap, and so on. Try to convey these gestures in your portrait, even more so than getting the features in correct proportion — this kind of observation is vital in capturing the "essence" of a person. Is your sitter a sprightly old lady with a cheerful smile and a twinkle in her eye, or is she small, frail and vulnerable with a wistful expression? Do you want to portray your uncle surrounded by momentoes of his past, or are you more interested in the way the light emphasizes the texture and topography of his face? Each person will demand a different approach in terms of the pose, lighting and background. Once you've decided *what* you want to say about your sitter, and *how* to say it, you will find the painting easier and more enjoyable.

Right: Strong directional light from one side skimmed across the surface of this man's features, revealing the wrinkles and folds of the skin. Zsuzsi Roboz drew the portrait boldly and decisively, leaving areas of bare paper to indicate the light-struck parts of the face.

This apparently relaxed and informal portrait of the artist's father was in fact carefully planned at the outset, with everything in the picture contributing to the character and mood of the subject. Here the artist, Lucy Willis, describes the development of the painting.

"My first decision was to place the figure off-centre and devote the rest of the canvas to the interior, every detail of which has been familiar to me since childhood. We lifted the lid of the piano so as to provide a dark background that emphasized my father's white hair, illuminated by light from the window on the left. I got him to look toward another window on the right so that his eyes reflected the light. The hands, those of an artist and sculptor, are a significant part of my father's character, so I made

sure they were posed prominently.

"I had prepared my canvas in advance with a warm pinky colour made up of palette scrapings and turpentine, rubbed in with a rag. When this was dry, I loosely drew in the figure and background with thin paint in a dark earth colour.

"I blocked in the main tones around the head (dark mixtures of Prussian blue, alizarin crimson and burnt sienna) and then concentrated on the face until I had a reasonable likeness. I used cool, light blues and mauves in the beard and skin, contrasted with reds and oranges (cadmium red and yellow, either pure or with touches of blue added to make browns). For the brightly lit hair I used white, with sometimes a hint of cadmium yellow.

"I decided that a second figure was needed to balance the composition and persuaded my

mother to stand at the window for a short time. The sun shone for a brief period through the doorway from a window beyond so I quickly mapped in the shadows it created on the floor. I mixed various neutral, sludgy colours for the foreground, and paler ones for the walls, and allowed a certain amount of the pink underpainting to show through in places. I only did the minimum of work on the face at this stage and did not touch it again afterward.

"I did a final tightening up of the drawing, working more closely on the patterns and textures. I also heightened the highlights with white, sometimes with blue, violet, yellow or red added, and deepened the darks on the shoes, piano and clothing. By the end of the fourth sitting I decided it was time to stop, before the painting became overworked."

DOUBLE AND GROUP PORTRAITS

Everyday scenes of family life are an enjoyable and rewarding subject to paint. People absorbed in some activity – a mother nursing her child, friends or family sitting together at the kitchen table – make a refreshing change from the more formal, head-and-shoulders portrait, and the implied relationship between the figures adds a further dimension to the image.

If you are presented with a request to paint a portrait consisting of a number of people, rather than an individual, you should never be afraid to tackle it. The artistic challenge is greater, but so are the possibilities for creating an exciting composition based around the inter-relationships that exist both between the individual members of the group, and the group itself and the setting.

Left: Susan Ryder painted these two young friends while they were dressing to go out for the evening. To prevent the standing girl from fading into the background, the artist asked her to look directly ahead, so that the eye is drawn to her face. Ryder was also fascinated by the combination of warm lamplight in the room and the cool daylight coming in from the window.

Planning the portrait

A successful group portrait shows every member to advantage, yet forms a pleasing arrangement when viewed as a whole. The secret is to plan in advance: first think about the overall structure of the picture – its colour scheme, the lighting, background and props, and the arrangement and distribution of the figures – and then work on the pose and appearance of each individual. It's also a good idea to make several preliminary sketches, both of individual figures and of the whole group, and to take photographs for reference. These will not only help you to plan the composition, they will also come in useful at a later stage; since it is unlikely that you will complete the portrait in one sitting, these sketches and photos will give you the visual information you need to carry on with the painting between sittings if you wish.

Arranging the group

People tend to form cohesive groups naturally, especially if they are family or friends, and it is often best to start out by asking your sitters simply to relax together and feel at ease, while you make sketches and take note of how individuals react to each other and the gestures and poses they adopt naturally. If all goes well, you may find that with just a little "fine-tuning" – moving a hand here, tilting a head there – you are ready to proceed with the painting. On the other hand, the positions adopted by individuals may not add up to a satisfactory composition: watch out in particular for awkwardly placed hands, arms that hang limply, and heads that are all on the same level, leading to monotony. (You'll find that looking at the group through a camera lens or a carboard viewfinder will immediately bring these faults to your attention because distracting background details are eliminated.)

The arrangement of the figures in a group portrait can add to the narrative interest of the picture. By positioning the figures in certain positions – looking at each other, back to back, hands touching – you are saying something about the people and the situation. Try out several compositions on a small scale first and experiment by positioning the subjects in different ways to see how this affects the

Above: This family portrait by Ian Sidaway contains a variety of head height, pose and expression, which adds interest to the shape of the group.

relationship between them. For example, a double portrait in which one person is facing you and one is in profile will convey a different message to one in which two people face each other. To emphasize a close-knit group, overlap some figures and arrange limbs and hands to create body contact between members of the group.

Background and props

You can tell the viewer a great deal about any group of people simply by choosing props and background that set a mood and underline the apparent relationship between the figures. For example, a domestic setting for a family group emphasizes their informal bond, while for a group of business people a more formal setting, including perhaps a desk, or a window with a view of a city skyline, might be appropriate.

SELF-PORTRAITS

The self-portrait is one of the enduring traditions of Western art. Many great masters, among them Rembrandt, Rubens, van Gogh and Cézanne, have produced some of their most revealing work through their self-portraits. Rembrandt painted over sixty of them, recording his decline from proud youth to lonely old age.

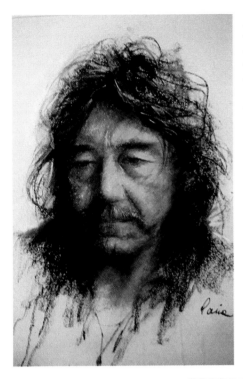

A valuable way of learning and experimenting for the portrait painter is to draw or paint self-portraits. It is only through trial and error that we learn to avoid mistakes, and only through frequent practise that we can develop a facility for depicting, quickly and accurately, the features of the face. But not everyone — not even long-suffering members of your own family — is prepared to sit patiently for long periods while you practise and experiment. The least they'll expect out of it is a flattering portrait. In yourself, on the other hand, you have a model who is available at any time, endlessly patient — and who won't be offended if the finished portrait is less than flattering!

As a model, you will be relaxed and unselfconscious; as a painter, you are free to express an honest, warts-and-all response to your subject. This in turn will foster a congenial atmosphere in which your painting style and technique can develop naturally.

Try out a number of poses and expressions, lighting set-ups and backgrounds, and make several sketches before starting to paint. Three-quarter views are the most convenient for self-portraits, as it is easy to work from mirror to easel without moving your head too much. Sit comfortably with a good light on one side and with a mirror 1.2–1.5m (4–5ft) away from you. Remember that aspects such as composition, colour and tonal balance are just as important in the finished portrait as achieving a likeness.

Left: In this pastel self-portrait Ken Paine has employed selective focus to good effect. The head is painted solidly with careful use of light and shade and the hair, finished carelessly, achieves an exciting contrast to the more formalized portrayal of the features.

Opposite page: This is one of a series of self-portraits which John Plumb has made over the years, recording his development as an artist. Free from the pressures associated with painting someone else's portrait, he was able to treat his own portrait as an exploration of technique, colour and composition; the making of the painting was more important than "getting a likeness". He began with an underpainting, then painted the face in just three tones. When this was, dry he refined the tones and colours with transparent glazes. Plumb worked on the painting over a period of months, returning to it at intervals to adjust the composition until he felt that the "architecture" of the painting was right.

Right: An interesting aspect of self-portraiting is that you are treating your own face as if it belongs to another, but at the same time you are privileged with a depth of self-knowledge. In this charcoal self-portrait, Zsuzsi Roboz seeks out aspects of mood and personality.

PORTRAITS OUTDOORS

Working outdoors presents several new challenges to the artist, and the unpredictability of the weather is one of them. You'll find plenty of opportunity to exploit interesting backgrounds and settings, as well as the play of sunlight and shadow on the sitter's face and figure.

Some sitters find the atmosphere of a studio, or even a room, too inhibiting to be able to relax and adopt a natural pose. They may feel more at ease sitting in their own garden, which somehow seems less "formal". And if your sitter happens to be a natural "outdoors" type, it might be fun to paint him or her in a favourite setting, whether it be fishing on a river bank, messing about on a boat, pottering in the garden, or togged up ready for riding or tennis. Outdoor portraits have a refreshing informality and allow you to present your sitter in an active, rather than passive, pose.

Outdoor light lends sparkle and animation to a portrait, but its drawback is that it can produce unsightly and unflattering shadows, and — even worse — make the subject squint. The solution is to place the sitter with the sun behind him, or in an area of open shade. The ideal conditions for an outdoor portrait are provided by a slightly overcast sky, producing a diffused, kind light. Unlike bright sunlight, overcast light is an even source of illumination and usually remains consistent throughout the day, enabling painting sessions to last several hours.

Be sure also to set up your easel and palette in the shade. If you paint in bright sunlight, you'll find it difficult to judge tones and colours accurately and they may be distorted — as you'll discover when you later take your painting indoors.

Painting outdoor portraits involves a race against time, because the quality of the light changes and shadows move as the day progresses. If your portrait extends to more than one session it is best to restrict yourself to an hour or two on the first day and continue working when the same conditions again prevail. Alternatively, you could take photographs and make preliminary sketches of your sitter, using a fast medium such as pastel or watercolour, and work up the painting in oils later, indoors.

Above: This oil portrait by Lucy Willis explores the effect of light filtering through leaves and reflecting on the sitter's face and clothing and on the ground. The shadowy face is flushed with luminous colour, caused by a combination of cool light reflected from the sky and warm light reflected upward from the model's clothing and from the book on her lap. To catch the effect of sunlight, it is crucial to keep your lights and shadows clearly defined. Observe how the really dark accents — in the doorway and on the girl's clothes — accentuate the high-key colours in the rest of the painting.

Above: A good portrait reveals something of the character of the subject from his expression, but by using a relevant background you can enlarge on this to show more of his way of life. Stephen Crowther painted his gardener at work outdoors, giving the portrait an extra element that would be lacking in the studio.

Left: Ian Sidaway painted this family group in front of their newly-built studio (designed by Piers Gough to look as though it has been torn open at the roof). The artist worked from separate photographs of each person – and the dog – piecing the group together back at his studio.

WORKING FROM PHOTOGRAPHS

Photographs can be an extremely useful aid to the portrait painter, provided they are used for information and guidance, rather than being slavishly copied. Many great artists of the past and present have used photographs as source material, from Delacroix, Sickert, Degas and Picasso to Andy Warhol, Richard Hamilton and the American photo-realist painters.

While there is no substitute for drawing and direct observation, a camera can be a helpful and time-saving tool when approaching a portrait. A Polaroid camera is particularly useful, as the pictures are produced instantly, and you can use them instead of sketches when deciding on a suitable pose or background and in arranging the composition. The camera will also record instantly a fleeting expression, or an interesting effect of light and shadow, which you can then translate at your leisure in a finished painting or drawing. Photographs can also be used as reference when painting clothing and background detail. This means that you can work on the painting after your sitter has gone home for the day, thus avoiding the necessity for long, tiring sittings. And, if a model isn't available, you can practise your technique by working from a photograph, or you may come across an interesting photograph in a newspaper or magazine which you'd like to use as inspiration for the composition of a portrait.

Photography, however, does have certain limitations. The camera can indeed lie, or at any rate distort the truth about colours, shapes and tones, and about perspective and spatial relationships. Another drawback if you work too directly from photographs is that the finished drawing or painting may be too static. Try to work in a loose, spontaneous manner, injecting movement, life and your own style into the image. Remember, too, that a camera is not selective — it records everything — and you must make a conscious decision about which elements of the image should be emphasized and which played down or omitted altogether.

Photography can be a useful tool for the portrait painter, but never, never be tempted to paint someone's portrait by working only from a photograph. Only by working direct from life can you hope to capture something of the model's spirit.

Left: Roy Herrick based this painting on a photograph he saw in an old newspaper. He was intrigued by the composition of the figures, reminiscent of a painting by Degas.

Top: Stephen Crowther painted this group portrait of friends and family enjoying a meal *al fresco* while on holiday in Venice. He took several photos of the group and the background buildings (**above and right**); the final image is a composite of elements taken from each of them and put together to form a pleasing composition.

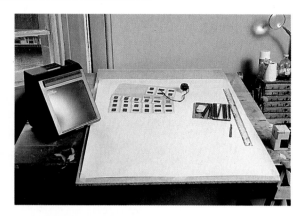

Ian Sidaway uses his camera as the equivalent of a sketchbook, and keeps a large reference file of transparencies which frequently spark off ideas for paintings. However, he never copies one photograph, but combines elements from several to create a new "hybrid" composition. This composition is fairly straightforward, but by placing the figures well down in the picture the artist emphasizes the youthful, carefree mood of the portrait. It is interesting to see how he viewed the development of the painting.

"The subjects of my painting were both keen football fans, so it seemed appropriate to portray them, proudly wearing their team scarves, outside Hammersmith football ground. Combining information from two photographs — one of the boys and one of the entrance to the football ground — I put together a composition in which the background was an integral part of the portrait.

"The working drawing was executed using a range of pencils and graphite sticks. I then squared up the drawing (see page 56) to enable me to transfer the image accurately onto the canvas.

"In a slightly unusual approach, I completed the background before starting on the figures.

"The figures were painted next, beginning with the faces and working downwards. I developed the image piece by piece, working back to blend the colours into each other.

"When the painting was dry I reworked some of the colours, strengthening shadows and altering tones until I was happy with the result."

STORAGE AND PRESENTATION

Having taken the trouble to create your drawings and paintings, it makes sense to look after them. Works on paper are particularly vulnerable to damage by dust, grease, damp and harsh sunlight, so ensure that they are stored safely until they can be given the further protection of framing.

Oil paintings

An oil painting doesn't have to be varnished, but a light coating will protect the paint surface from dust and moisture as well as giving it a uniform finish that brings the whole painting together. There is a wide choice of commercially prepared varnishes available, that give either a glossy or a semi-matt finish. However, varnish can only be applied when the painting is completely dry, which can take anything from six to 12 months, depending on the thickness of the paint. Retouching varnish can be applied when the paint is touch-dry and will protect the surface until it is dry enough for final varnishing.

Watercolours

When a watercolour painting is finished and dry, and if it has been stretched (see page 20) it must be cut from the board to which it is taped. This requires caution. The edges should be cut with a scalpel, but in doing this the released tension is so great that the paper may tear. To avoid this, cut opposite ends of the paper rather than working around the paper with your knife.

If your paintings cannot be framed straight away, store them flat in a large drawer in a dry, dust-free place.

Pastels and drawings

Pastel, chalk, Conté crayon and charcoal are all powdery media which smudge easily, and drawings should not be left unprotected for long. To guard against smearing, drawings can be fixed with a spray fixative which forms a thin, transparent coating. Store unframed drawings in a large drawer or artists' portfolio, interleaving the sheets with waxed paper, cellophane or tissue paper.

Framing

A well-chosen frame will not only enhance the appearance of your works but also protect and conserve them. There is a vast array of frame mouldings available, from the deep, ornately carved ones to simple metal, plastic or wooden strips. The choice is yours, but there are certain aesthetic points to consider when choosing a frame and your selection can make or mar the appearance of your picture. Most importantly, the frame should not be so eye-catching that it attracts more attention than the painting itself. When in doubt, it is better to opt for something that is discreetly formal.

Drawings, watercolours and pastels are normally framed under glass to protect them from dust and damp. The glass must be kept from contact with the surface of the work, to prevent smearing and the build-up of condensation, and so the picture is set in a card window mount/mat which acts as a buffer between picture and glass so the two don't touch. Mounting/matting a picture also gives it an aesthetically pleasing border that separates the image from the hard edge of the frame. Sometimes a thin coloured line may be drawn around the inside edge of the mount. This softens the edge of the mount and gives dignity and emphasis to the image.

GLOSSARY

Alla prima From the Italian for "at first". A direct method of painting in which an image is completed at one sitting, without preliminary underpainting or drawing.

Atmosphere In painting, "atmosphere" refers to the feeling of space and distance between foreground and background.

Blending A means of merging two colours or tones together, with a brush, rag, torchon or fingertip, so that no sharp divisions are visible.

Blocking in Applying broad masses of tone and colour in the early stages of a painting to establish the general composition and obliterate the ground.

Brights Short, stiff, square-tipped brushes that make precise, rectangular strokes. They are ideal for creating strongly textured impasto effects.

Broken colour A technique of applying paint in a pure state to the support instead of mixing it on the palette. The paint is applied in short strokes, next to and on top of one another, so breaking up the surface into tiny patches of colour. The use of broken colour was an important feature of Impressionism.

Chiaroscuro Derived from Italian meaning literally "light-dark". The term was used originally in reference to oil paintings with dramatic tonal contrasts. It is now more generally applied to the skilful exploitation of light and shadow within a painting or drawing. Rembrandt and Caravaggio are the artists particularly associated with the use of *chiaroscuro*.

Cold-pressed Paper with a very pronounced tooth. The rough surface makes lines appear broken and ragged, and tones flecked. Particularly used for large, bold watercolours.

Colour temperature The degree of warmth (toward red and orange) or coolness (toward blue and green) that a colour suggests in relation to other colours.

Complementary colours Each of the three primary colours has a complementary colour which is made by mixing the other two primaries. For instance, the complementary colour of red is green, a mixture of yellow and blue. When juxtaposed, complementary colours enhance and intensify one another.

Composition The sensitive and balanced arrangement of shapes, forms and colours in an image.

Crosshatching A technique of producing tonal and textural effects by building up a mass of criss-crossed strokes rather than by solid shading. Commonly associated with ink, pastel and pencil work, the technique can also be used in painting.

Dipper A small container with an open top for holding oil or turpentine ready to mix into oil colours to give them the desired consistency. Can be clipped onto the side of the palette.

Drybrush A technique in which the moisture is squeezed from the brush before being loaded with fairly dry, thick paint. This is then dragged or skimmed quickly across the surface of a painting so that the paint is left only on raised points, to create a textured, broken stroke.

Earth colours The range of pigments obtained from natural clays – various iron ores and oxides. They include the ochres, siennas, umbers, Indian red and terre verte. They are all permanent.

Fat A term describing pigment mixed with oil to make a thick paste, most often used in the later stages of a painting.

Fat-over-lean principle A traditional rule in oil painting whereby the underpainting is produced with "lean" paint – paint diluted with a large proportion of turpentine. As additional layers of paint are added to the canvas, so the oil content is increased, the "fattest" paint being applied last of all. This procedure helps to produce a resilient and flexible paint surface that will not crack.

Feathering A pastel technique for mixing colours by softly applying strokes of colour on top of one another. It ties the painting together and subtly changes its hue.

Ferrule The metal part of a paintbrush that holds the bristles in place.

Filberts Oil painting brushes with thin, slightly tapered tips and fuller middles, giving soft, full strokes.

Flats Oil painting brushes with long, thin bristles and square tips. They make precise, smooth strokes and fine lines.

Focal point The centre of interest in a painting or drawing.

Foreshortening The optical distortion of forms so that they appear shortened when viewed from an end-on position.

Fugitive colours Used to describe colours that are liable to fade in the course of time. This quality is usually indicated in code on paint tube labels.

Glazing An oil painting technique of applying thin, fluid layers of transparent paint wet-on-dry to produce luminous, glowing colours. A glaze can also be applied over opaque colour to enrich and modify it.

Half-tones The levels of shade in an image between the lightest and darkest tone, that is not a solid colour. The effect of half-tones is to soften tonal transitions and so suggest three-dimensional objects in space.

Hatching A technique of creating areas of tone in a drawing with fine, parallel strokes in a single direction. The closer the strokes the darker the tone.

Highlights The areas in a composition where the light is most intense.

Hot-pressed A smooth-surfaced, hard paper suitable for detailed, precise work with fine, unbroken lines.

Impasto Paint applied very thickly with a brush or knife to create a rough, uneven texture and a three-dimensional quality to the surface.

Key The prevailing tone of a painting or drawing. A predominantly light image is said to have a high key, a predominantly dark one a low key.

Lean A term describing pigment that has been thinned with turpentine so that it dries quickly and is ideal for underpainting.

Masking fluid A quick-drying solution – usually white – that is brushed over areas of a painting that are to remain unpainted. Colour can be applied over the areas masked by the fluid. The dried mask is rubbed off with an eraser or finger once the surrounding areas are dry.

Medium In painting and drawing, this term is used in two ways: to refer to the material in which a painting or drawing is executed – oil, watercolour, pencil, etc. – (pl. media); or to the substance with which pigment is mixed to make it flow – oil in oil paint, etc. – (pl. mediums).

Modelling Expressing the volume and solidity of an object by using tonal variations to depict areas of light and shade on an object or figure.

Monochrome underpainting The first stage of a painting, executed in thin paint, that is a tonal version or sketch of the finished work. Starting with one is a good way to establish forms in terms of light and shade before introducing colour and detail.

Mop A watercolour brush with a full, round head of bristles, useful for laying large washes.

Negative space Generally, this refers to the background of a picture – the space surrounding the principal subject. While not the main focus, it should still be interesting and balanced with the "positive" shapes.

Not Also known as cold-pressed, a medium-textured paper whose surface breaks up lines and tones just enough to give them character.

Permanent When applied to paints this refers to their ability to retain their colour without fading in normal atmospheric conditions.

Priming A treatment applied to canvas or board which makes the surface non-absorbent and suitable for painting on.

Renaissance The intellectual and artistic movement that began in Italy around the beginning of the 15th century, based on reviving and re-interpreting classical Greek culture. The term comes from the French for "rebirth". The movement reached its peak during the early 16th century, in the work of artists such as Raphael, Michelangelo and da Vinci.

Round A thin, long-bristled brush that tapers slightly at the end. Round brushes are equally suited to filling in details or covering large areas.

Scumbling A technique of spreading a veil of semi-opaque colour loosely and unevenly across the paint surface so that the colour underneath shows through in places.

Sfumato Tones blended with imperceptibly subtle transitions. The word is Italian for "evaporated". Leonardo da Vinci was the most famous exponent of this technique.

Tone The degree of lightness or darkness in a colour. Every colour's inherent tone is also modified by the effect of the available light source.

Tooth The degree of roughness or texture of a canvas or paper surface. It determines how well the paint or drawing medium adheres to the surface. In general, a pronounced tooth is better for bold, large-scale work and a fine tooth for detailed pictures.

Torchon A pencil-like roll of tightly wrapped paper with tapered ends, used to blend and smooth tones of pencil, charcoal or pastel marks into one another.

Wash A very dilute transparent layer of colour which is applied loosely and broadly to a surface. Usually associated with water-based media such as watercolour.

Watermark The symbol or name of the manufacturer incorporated in sheets of high-quality watercolour paper. The watermark is visible when the paper is held up to the light.

Wet-in-wet A method of painting in which one layer of wet, fluid colour is applied over another and mixed directly on the painting surface. Tones and colours can be subtly blended and fused to achieve a soft effect.

Wet-on-dry Applying paint to a colour that has been allowed to dry thoroughly, in order to achieve crisp shapes and controlled brushstrokes.

INDEX

Page numbers in *italic* refer to the illustrations and captions

A
Alice, Princess, *92*
alla prima, 11, *46*, 48, 50, *50*, 108
Andrea del Sarto, 27
Antonello da Messina, 10
arms, 34
Artists' colours, 14, 18
Artists' "donkeys", 29, *29*
Atherton, Barry, *47*, *59*
atmosphere, 108

B
backgrounds, 66–9, 97, 100, *101*
backlighting, *72*, 74
Bacon, Francis, *81*
balance, 69
beards, *41*
blending colours, 59, *59*, 60, 108
blocking in, 108
boards, 17
Bond, Jane, *89*
Bowyer, William, *43*
brights, 14, 108
bristle brushes, *13*, 14
broken colour, 51, *51*, 108
Bruce, George J. D., *41*, *67*, *77*
brushes, *13*, 14
    cleaning, 14, 19
    for watercolours, 19, *20*

C
canvases, *16–17*, 17, 48
Caravaggio, 10, 108
Carrigan, Marian, *81*
Cézanne, Paul, 98
chalks, 27, 59–60, 106
charcoal, 22–3, *23*, 56, *56*, 106
Charles, Prince of Wales, *45*
chiaroscuro, 10, *75*, 108
children, *54*, *65*, 88–9, *88–91*

Classicism, 11
cleaning brushes, 14, 19
clothing, 76–7, *76–7*
cold-pressed paper, 20, 108
coloured pencils, *26*, 27, 59, *60*
colours: backgrounds, 66–9
    blending, 59–60, *59*
    choosing, 14
    complementary, 108
    flesh tones, 46–7, *46–7*, 60
    optical mixing, *49*, 51, 59–60
    pastels and crayons, 25, 59–60
    temperature, 108
    watercolours, 18–19
complementary colours, 108
composition, 66–9, *66–9*, 97, 108
Conté crayons, *26*, 27, *27*, 106
cotton canvas, 17
counterchange, *11*
craft knives, 23
crayons, 26–7, *26–7*, 58–61, 106
crosshatching, *56*, 57, 60, *60*, 108
Crowther, Stephen, *65*, *74*, *101*
Cubism, 11

D
David, Madeleine, *60*
Degas, Edgar, 24, 100
Delacroix, Eugène, 100
diffused lighting, 74
dippers, 14–17, 108
"donkeys", 29, *29*
double portraits, 96–7, *96*
drawing boards, 29
drybrush, *54*, 55, 108
Dürer, Albrecht, 10, 40

E
ears, 34, *38*, 39–40
earth colours, 108
easels, 28–9, *28–9*

Edwards, John, *36*, *38*
England, 10
equipment, 12–29
erasers, 23, *23*, 56, 57
Expressionism, 11
Eyck, Jan van, 8–10, *8*
eyebrows, *41*
eyes, 33–4, 36–7, *36*, 69

F
facial features, 33–4, 36–41, *36–41*
fan blender brushes, *20*
fat, 108
"fat over lean", 48, 108
Fauves, 11
feathering, 61, *61*, 108
features, 33–4, 36–41, *36–41*
ferrules, 108
filberts, 14, 108
fixatives, 22, *25*, 106
Flanders, 8
flat washes, watercolours, 53
flats, 14, 108
flesh tones, 46–7, *46–7*, 60
focal points, 108
folds, in clothing, 77, *77*
foreshortening, 71, 108
form and volume, 34–5
format, *68*, 69
Foster, Richard, *49*, *66*
framing, 106
fugitive colours, 18–19, 108

G
Gainsborough, Thomas, 7, 10, *10*
Giotto di Bondone, 8
glazing, 10, 47, *49*, 50, 108
Glehn, Wilfrid Gabriel de, *63*
Gogh, Vincent van, 50, 98
Gough, Piers, *101*
graded washes, *52*, 53
Graham, David, *34*
graphite pencils, 23, *23*
Greece, 8
Greenman, Edwin, *76*, *93*
grids, squaring up, *67*, *67*
grounds, toned, 48

group portraits, 96–7, *96–7*, *101*
gum turpentine, 14

H
hair, 40–1, *40–1*
half-tones, 109
Hamilton, Richard, 100
hands, 34, 42, *42–3*, 69, 71
Hankey, William Lee, *54*
hatching, *56*, 57, 60, *60*, 109
heads, 32–5, *32–5*
Hepple, Norman, *71*
Herrick, Roy, *100*
highlights, *36*, 37, 47, 55, *56*, 57, 109
Hilliard, Nicholas, 7
history, 8–11
Hockney, David, 27
Hogarth, William, 10
hog's hair brushes, *13*, 14
Holbein, Hans, 10
Hope, Sally, *54*, *74*, *89*
hot-pressed paper, 20, 109
Hunter, David, *72*
Hutchinson, Mr and Mrs John, *11*

I
impasto, 10, 14, 50, *50*, *77*, 109
Impressionism, 47, 51
informal portraits, 78, *78–9*
Ingres, Dominique, 10–11, *10*
irises, eyes, 36, *36*
Italy, 8, 10

K
key, 109
kneadable erasers, 23, *23*, 56, 57
knives, 14, 23

L
lean, 109
Leonardo da Vinci, 7, 10, 92, 109
lighting, 41, 72–4, *72–5*, 85, 89, 100
likenesses, 44–5, *44–5*

linen canvas, 17
linseed oil, 14
lips, 37–9, *37*

M
mahl sticks, 17, *51*
masking fluid, 55, 109
materials, 12–29
mediums, 14, 109
men, 84–5, *84–7*
Michelangelo, 10, 27, 109
Midgley, Julia, *61*
modelling, 109
monochrome
   underpainting, 48, 109
mood, 72
Moore, George, *11*
mops, *20*, 109
Morris, Anthony, *46, 50*
mounts/mats, 106
moustaches, *41*
mouths, 33, 37–9, *37*, 45

N
necks, 34
negative space, 66, 109
Netherlands, 8
Noakes, Michael, *44, 45, 92*
noses, *39*, 40
Not paper, 20, 109
nylon brushes, 14, 19

O
oil paints, 10, 14, 48–51,
   49–51, 106
oil pastels, 25, *25*
older people, 92–3, *92–5*
optical mixing, 49, 51, 59–60
outdoor portraits, 100,
   100–1
ox hair brushes, 19

P
Paine, Ken, *31, 41, 58, 74,
   74, 75, 89, 93, 99*
painting knives, 14
paints: oil, 14, 48–51, *49–51*
   watercolours, 18–19,
   18–19, 52–5, *52–5*
palette knives, 14
palettes, 14

paper: for oils, *16, 17*
   for pastels and crayons,
   25, 59
   stretching, *20–1*, 21
   watercolour, 19–21, *21*
pastels, 24–5, *24–5*, 58–61,
   58–9, 61, 106
Pears Soaps, *90–1*
pencils, 23, 56–7, *56*
   charcoal, 22, *23*
   coloured, *26*, 27, 59, *60*
   pastel, 24
   sharpening, 23
   as sighting tools, *32, 33,
   34, 44*
   water-soluble, *26*, 27
permanent colours, 18–19,
   109
photographic references,
   89, 97, 100, *101*, 102,
   102–5
Picasso, Pablo, 7, 100
pigments, 14, 24
Pissarro, Lucien, *40*
Pliny, 8
Plumb, John, *98*
Polaroid cameras, 100
poses, 70–1, *70–1*, 85, 88
presentation, 106
priming, 109
profiles, *33*, 34
propelling pencils, 23, *23*
proportions, *32*, 33, 44, 69
props, 97
putty erasers, 23, 56, 57

R
radial easels, 28–9, *28*
Raphael, 10, 109
reflected light, 74
Rembrandt lighting, 74, *75*,
   85
Rembrandt van Rijn, 7, 10,
   40, 48, 92, 98, 108
Renaissance, 8, 67, 109
Renoir, Pierre Auguste, 30,
   47
Reynolds, Sir Joshua, 10
Rizvi, Jacqueline, *55*
Roboz, Zsuzsi, *42, 56, 64,
   70, 71, 79, 85, 93, 99*

Romans, 8
round brushes, 14, *20*, 109
Rubens, Peter Paul, 48, 98
"rule of thirds", 69
Rutherford, Dame
   Margaret, *44*
Ryder, Susan, *53, 57, 68, 80,
   82–3, 84, 90–1, 96*

S
sable brushes, 14, 19
sanding blocks, *23*
Sargent, John Singer, *11*
scalpels, 23, *23*
scumbling, 49, 50, 61, *61*,
   109
self-portraits, 98–9, *98–9*
sfumato, 10, 56, 109
shadows, 41, 47, 72, 74
sharpening pencils, 23
shoulders, 34
Sickert, Walter Richard, 100
Sidaway, Ian, *51, 52, 55, 56,
   73, 86–7, 97, 101, 102–3*
side lighting, *72*, 74, 85
sketches, 64, *64–5*, 67, *67*,
   89, *91*
sketching easels, 28, 29
sketching paper, *17*
skin tones, 46–7, *46–7*, 60
sponges, *18*, 19
spotlights, 74
squaring up, 67, *67*
Steer, Philip Wilson, *11*
storage, 106
Strand, Sally, *79*
stretching paper, *20–1*, 21
Students' colours, 14, 18
studio easels, 28, *28*

T
table top easels, 29, *29*
teeth, 38–9
texture, 10
   canvases, 17
   clothing, *76–7, 77*
   drybrush, *54*, 55
   impasto, 50, *50*
   paper, 59
   skin, 47
   watercolour paper, 20–1

three-quarter lighting, 72–4,
   72, 74, 85
three-quarter poses, 8–10,
   33–4, *33*, 99
Todd, Daphne, *78*
tone, 109
toned grounds, 48
Tonks, Henry, *11*
"tooth", paper, 20, 109
torchons, 22–3, 109
Toulouse-Lautrec, Henri
   de, 27
turpentine, 14, 48

U
underpainting,
   monochrome, 48, 109

V
varnishes, 106
Velázquez, Diego de, 92
Venice, 10
Vermeer, Jan, *9*
volume, 34–5

W
Warhol, Andy, 100
washes: toned grounds, 48
   watercolour, 52–3, *52*, 55,
   109
water-soluble pencils, *26*,
   27
watercolours, 18–19, *18–19*,
   52–5, *52–5*
   brushes, 19, *20*
   paper, 19–21, *21*
   storage, 106
watermarks, 109
Watteau, Jean-Antoine, 27
weights, paper, 21
wet-into-wet, 50–1, *51*, 53–5,
   54, 55, 109
wet-over-dry, *53*, 54, 109
Whistler, J. A. M., 7, *69*
Willis, Lucy, *47, 51, 52, 61,
   70, 94–5*, 100
women, 80–1, *82–3*
Wright, Naomi, *85*

ACKNOWLEDGEMENTS

We would particularly like to thank Martha Allequen of the New Academy Gallery
and Business Art Galleries, London, for her generous assistance, also Annabel
Elton from the Federation of British Artists. Our thanks also to all the artists who
contributed their work so generously and especially Michael Noakes,
Susan Ryder and Zsuzsi Roboz.

Picture Credits

3	Susan Ryder, NEAC	60	Madeleine A.J. David
5	David Graham	61TL	Lucy Willis
6	Ken Paine	61B	Julia Midgley/New Academy Gallery and Business Art Galleries
8	The National Gallery, London		
9	National Gallery of Art, Washington (Andrew W. Mellon Collection)	63	Wilfrid Gabriel de Glehn, RA/Photo: David Messum
		64L	Zsuzsi Roboz
10T	Courtauld Institute Galleries, London (Courtauld Collection)	64R	Zsuzsi Roboz
		65T	Stephen Crowther, ARCA, RBA
10B	Hubert Josse	65BL	from People of Importance by J.H. Dowd and Brenda E. Spender
11T	The Brooklyn Museum		
11B	The National Portrait Gallery, London	65BR	from People of Importance by J.H. Dowd and Brenda E. Spender
13	Daler-Rowney		
15	Daler-Rowney	66	Richard Foster/New Academy Gallery and Business Art Galleries
16–17	all pictures Daler-Rowney		
18–19	MB/Photo: Steve Tanner	67T	George J.D. Bruce, VPRP
20–21	MB/Photo: Steve Tanner	67B	George J.D. Bruce, VPRP
21R	Daler-Rowney	68	Susan Ryder, NEAC
22–23	MB/Photo: Steve Tanner	69	Barber Institute of Fine Arts, Birmingham
24–25	MB/Photo: Steve Tanner	70T	Zsuzsi Roboz
26–27	MB/Photo: Steve Tanner	70B	Lucy Willis
27T	Jacqueline L. Rizvi, RWS	71T	Zsuzsi Roboz
28–29	Winsor & Newton	71B	Norman Hepple, RA, PPRP/New Academy Gallery and Business Art Galleries
31	Ken Paine		
34T	George J.D. Bruce, VPRP	72	David Hutter
34C	George J.D. Bruce, VPRP	73	Ian Sidaway
34B	David Graham	74TL	Sally Hope/New Academy Gallery and Business Art Galleries
35	George J.D. Bruce, VPRP		
36	John Edwards, RP	74TR	Ken Paine
37	from People of Importance by J.H. Dowd and Brenda E. Spender	74B	Stephen Crowther, ARCA, RBA
		75	Ken Paine
38	John Edwards, RP	76	Edwin Greenman, ARCA, RP, FRSA
40	Visual Arts Library	77	George J.D. Bruce, VPRP
41TL	Ken Paine	78	Daphne Todd, RP, NEAC
41TR	Ken Paine	79T	Zsuzsi Roboz
41B	George J.D. Bruce, VPRP	79B	Sally Strand
42	Zsuzsi Roboz	80	Susan Ryder, NEAC
43TL	Ian Sidaway	81T	MB/Photo: Angelo Hornak
43TR	William Bowyer/Metrographic Arts	81B	Marian Carrigan
44	Michael Noakes, PPROI, RP. Study for a portrait of Dame Margaret Rutherford, DBE. In the collection of the National Portrait Gallery, London. Pencil 1970	83	Susan Ryder, NEAC
		84	Susan Ryder, NEAC
		85T	Zsuzsi Roboz
		85B	Naomi C. Wright
45	Michael Noakes, PPROI, RP. Drawing of HRH The Prince of Wales, made in connection with the portrait commissioned by the 2nd King Edward VII's Own Gurkhas. Pencil July 1983	86–87	all pictures Ian Sidaway
		88	Jane Bond/New Academy Gallery and Business Art Galleries
		88–89	Sally Hope/New Academy Gallery and Business Art Galleries
46	Anthony Morris, RP		
47T	Barry Atherton/New Academy Gallery and Business Art Galleries	89	Ken Paine
		90–91	Susan Ryder, NEAC
47B	Lucy Willis	92	Michael Noakes, PPROI, RP. HRH Princess Alice, Countess of Athlone. Study for Portrait. Oil 20" × 24" 1978–79
49	Richard Foster/New Academy Gallery and Business Art Galleries		
50	Anthony Morris, RP	93TL	Edwin Greenman, ARCA, RP, FRSA
51T	Lucy Willis	93TR	Ken Paine
51B	Ian Sidaway	93B	Zsuzsi Roboz
52TL	Ian Sidaway	94–95	all pictures Lucy Willis
52TR	Lucy Willis	96	Susan Ryder, NEAC
53	Susan Ryder, NEAC	97	Ian Sidaway
54T	Sally Hope/New Academy Gallery and Business Art Galleries	98	John Plumb
		99T	Ken Paine
54B	William Lee Hankey/Chris Beetles Gallery, London	99B	Zsuzsi Roboz
		100	Lucy Willis
55BL	Ian Sidaway	101T	Stephen Crowther, ARCA, RBA
55BR	Jacqueline L. Rizvi, RWS	101B	Ian Sidaway
56TL	Zsuzsi Roboz	102	Roy Herrick
56TC	Ian Sidaway	103	all pictures Stephen Crowther, ARCA, RBA
58	Ken Paine	104–5	all pictures Ian Sidaway
59	Barry Atherton/New Academy Gallery and Business Art Galleries	106–7	MB/Photo: Peter Marshall